Opening the New Testament

Opening the New Testament

By FLOYD V. FILSON

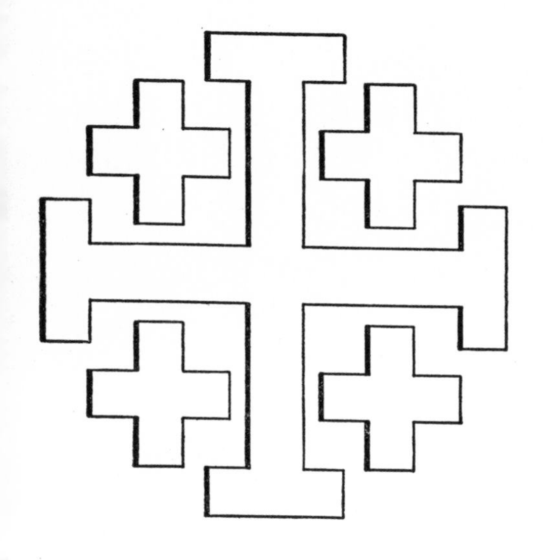

The Westminster Press
PHILADELPHIA

Library of Congress Catalogue Card Number: 52-7116

Printed in the United States of America

Contents

Opening the New Testament

CHAPTER 1

The Story They Told

TWO MEN stood on trial before the Jewish rulers. What had they done? They had preached a new message about Jesus of Nazareth. In his name they had shown amazing power to heal a lame man in the Temple, and the rulers were indignant that these simple men, without official authority, presumed to teach and act in the Temple itself. They commanded both men to preach no more; but Peter and John said, "We cannot but speak of what we have seen and heard" (Acts 4: 20) . . .

A man named Stephen stood before the Jewish leaders in Jerusalem. He too had preached this same message. Men opposed him, but "they could not resist the wisdom and the Spirit with which he spoke" (Acts 6: 10). So they seized him and brought him before the leaders. When he refused to apologize or give up his faith, the crowd dragged him from the city and stoned him. As he died, he prayed for them, "Lord, do not hold this sin against them" (Acts 7: 60) . . .

The friends of Paul were warning him that prison awaited him if he went on to take a collection to the needy Christians in Jerusalem. Paul knew already what it meant to be persecuted. He had been imprisoned, beaten with lash and rod, stoned, and driven from many a city by hostile mob or rulers. The warning, he well knew, was no idle threat. Yet he promptly said to his anxious friends, "I am ready not only to be imprisoned but even to die at Jerusalem for the name of the Lord Jesus" (Acts 21: 13) . . .

At Jerusalem not many days later, while Paul was in the Temple with Christian friends, a false accuser roused a mob against him. They seized him, beat him, and would have killed him had not the Roman guard rescued him. As the soldiers carried him to the steps that led into the soldiers' quarters, what was in Paul's mind? Was he eager to get into the barracks to be safe? No! As they carried him away, he begged the officer, "Let me speak to the people" (Acts 21: 39). He had but one desire: he wanted another chance to tell his story.

A New Teaching with Power

What was this story—this story that men could not keep from telling even at the cost of life itself?

It was the story back of our New Testament, the story that every New Testament writer presents in his own way. But before the New Testament books were collected, before even one of them had been written, the message they contain was already winning the loyalty and changing the lives of more and more people. At first they were few in numbers, and by the world's standards they were not great. Yet in spite of ridicule, imprisonment, beatings, and even stoning, they passed on from city to city to spread their message. Before they wrote it down, they told it, lived it, and suffered for it. So when they did write it, they wrote with the earnestness and power that had marked their telling of it all along.

God Acted in Christ

What was it, then, that these bold, persistent preachers said? They kept telling their hearers what God had done through one person. They did more than give rules for life or advice for people in trouble. What they did was to tell their story about Jesus of Nazareth. Though they told it in different ways, each preacher in his own way, they always spoke of Jesus as the central figure of their message and the most important figure of history. They did not shrink from claiming that, in this man, God himself had entered human life. They boldly declared that sooner or later every man must reckon with Jesus of Nazareth.

To most people outside of the group of Christians, Jesus seemed a person of no importance whatsoever. He was not a king, a high priest, a general, a rich man, or a world-famous scholar. To the leaders of his day he appeared to be a nobody. He held no official position, and while he came from a good home, his people were just a respectable, unpretentious family of an unimportant small town in despised Galilee. A member of a people subject to Rome, a carpenter's son of ordinary education who himself had worked with his hands for a living, he seemed to deserve no special attention or respect. And at the end of his career he seemed especially weak and unimpressive because, after his wandering life as a homeless teacher, the Roman rulers had crucified him on the complaint of the Jewish leaders! He had been put to death in the cruel, degrading manner reserved for rebels and criminals. He had seemed to be completely discredited.

Why, then, did the Christians so eagerly and gladly put their faith in Jesus? Why were they ready to suffer for this faith? They saw in him what others had not yet found. In him they saw God at work as never before. They told how "God anointed Jesus of Nazareth with the Holy Spirit and with power; how he went about doing good and healing all that were oppressed by the devil, for God was with him" (Acts 10:38). In his friendship to all classes, his teaching of all who would listen, his healing of the sick, his gathering of a brotherhood pledged to do God's will, they had seen the marks of a new work of God for men. So they had followed Jesus as their Master; they had become bound together in a new community of which he was the leader and head.

How could they do this when they knew that at the end of his life Jesus, disowned by the leaders of his people, had been crucified?

God Raised Him from the Dead

Here we come to the heart of what the first Christians said. Here we learn why the followers of Jesus carried forward his work with such faithfulness and power. The key to their message was that God had raised Jesus from the dead and made him the Lord of his Church. They did not follow a leader who had died and left them with nothing but the memory of his teaching and his brief life soon cut off. They did not follow a leader who had gone from them and left them to depend on their own strength. They served Jesus Christ the risen Lord, whom death could not hold down.

Now they saw all things in a new light. They had known during his ministry that Jesus was great and good; they had gladly believed that he was the greatest God-sent leader that his people had ever known. They had recognized his right to their full loyalty and service. When men crucified him, for a time they were confused and crushed. But when God raised him from the dead, they did more than recover their former faith. They now believed in their Master in a way that was impossible for them before. It became clear to them at last what God was doing through Jesus. And when God's Spirit came upon them at Pentecost, they had to speak of Jesus to the people. Then, for the first time, the full story could be told.

God Has Fulfilled His Promises

These apostles had a new message to preach. Nothing like the life, death, and resurrection of Jesus had ever happened before. Yet they, like Jesus himself (Matt. 5: 17), saw that his work carried on and fulfilled what God had done for Israel in the past. To people who were grateful for that past work of God the early Christian leaders came and said: "Jesus never disowned what your law and your prophets have said; he did not despise what God had already done; he came not to ignore or scorn the great acts and gifts of God to Israel, but to build upon them, to fulfill the divine promises made to early generations, to carry God's good purpose forward to victory."

This was a leading point in the first Christian preaching. In Jesus Christ God fulfilled his promises to Israel. The disciples had seen this in part even before the death and resurrection of Jesus. But once he was raised from the dead, they understood it far better. They gained a new understanding of the Scriptures of their people (our Old Testament); they read them with new interest, and used them in Christian preaching.

Through Christ, God Redeems His People

Before Jesus rose from the dead, what did the disciples hope he was going to do? On the evening of resurrection day, we are told, two disciples walked a lonely road, not knowing that Jesus had already risen. When a stranger overtook them, they did not recognize that it was Jesus himself, and to him they poured out their hopes and disappointments. "We had hoped," they said, "that he was the one to redeem Israel" (Luke 24: 21). But now, it seemed, it was not to be so.

Redeem Israel! What a world of meaning those words held for the Jewish people! They long had dreamed of how God would come and redeem—rescue, deliver—the people of Israel. They had thought that in some way God would save them from ill fortune and free them from the power of their enemies. They had thought that just as God had acted in ancient times to deliver them from the Egyptians, so he would act again to rescue them from calamity and suffering and usher in a new day for their nation. Many looked for a special servant or messenger of God—the Messiah, the Christ, the Anointed One—to come and save them from their troubles.

Before the end of the ministry of Jesus, his disciples discerned that he was the Christ they had expected (Mark 8: 27-30). After the crucifixion, it first appeared to them that Jesus was not, after all, the deliverer. But in the light of the resurrection, their eyes were opened and they saw that he had proved to be "the one to redeem Israel." In a sense deeper than they had expected, he was indeed their Christ and Redeemer. For he rescued men from the power of sin that spoils human life. In him they found forgiveness for all past wrong, and together with that the wisdom and strength to do right in the future. He opened up a new kind of life for those who believed in him. So to men burdened by a sense of their failures the apostles declared that through Jesus Christ life could be made over. He offered redemption from sin. The message that the disciples preached dealt with the troubles of men by striking at their root—the selfish sinfulness of the human heart and life.

The Cross Is God's Way to Victory

Now the disciples saw the real meaning of the life and death of Jesus. Before his death they sensed the power and greatness of his teaching, the strength of his humble life, his willingness to help the troubled people he met, and his strange power to heal the sick. Yet they never were free from the idea that his teaching and helpful life alone would be enough to establish a better day for man. They expected his sheer goodness to capture the conscience and loyalty of those who knew him. Why should it be necessary for him to *suffer?* When men crucified him, his disciples were tempted to feel that not only they but Jesus and even God himself had suffered defeat.

In the light of the resurrection they now knew better. They saw the truth of what Jesus, in his words and in his life, had been saying all the time: "God cares for his people; he comes to them in their need, even if they have done wrong; he acts to help them; he sends Jesus to do for them what they could not do for themselves; Jesus willingly takes the way of humble, costly living, the way of unselfish suffering, in order to do God's work and help God's children. This, and this alone, is the way of life that is truly great; this is the way of life that in God's world and by God's will is to triumph."

Before the resurrection, the disciples never really understood the greatness of costly living, of living for others instead of for oneself. They also failed to see how for Jesus this spirit of his life must lead him to give his life to accomplish God's work and meet men's need. The resurrection led them to see how fully God had been at work in him in all that he had done; it taught them that the way he took was God's way to reach and redeem men. So with the light that the resurrection shed on the ministry and death of Jesus, they told the entire story and what it meant for them and for others. Ministry, death, resurrection—it was all one story of the central person in whom God had been at work.

Jesus Christ Is Lord

But the Christians did not stop with a story about the past. That God had fulfilled his promises to Israel, that in Jesus he had been active to redeem men, was by no means all that they had to say. This risen Jesus is now "at the right hand of God" (Acts 2: 33); that is, he was raised to a position of power and authority and so was placed by God at the head of God's people. He is the Lord, the Lord of the Church, the Lord of each member of the people of God.

This means that he has the right to command the faith and obedience of *all* men—not only the Jews. For as the disciples realized that the risen Christ was head over all God's people, they came to recognize clearly that he had divine help to give to Jew and Gentile alike. He was the Lord not only of Israel but of all others as well.

Christ the Lord Will Judge All Men

And this Lordship, the Christian leaders declared, will finally be made clear to the whole creation at the last day. The early preachers not only told how God had fulfilled his promises in the work of Jesus and in the present Lordship of the risen Christ; they also had a message about the future. They spoke, therefore, of the coming completion of God's plan, and they expected that time rather soon. They told how Christ will carry God's cause to triumph and then judge all men at the end of the age. "He is the one ordained by God to be judge of the living and the dead" (Acts 10: 42).

Here is no ordinary person. Here is not just an unusual man. Here is a human life, but in it is the presence and work of God himself. Here is the central life of history, the greatest figure of all time, the person with whom every man must finally reckon. It is no wonder that in preaching this message of redemption given through Christ the disciples showed such earnestness, persistence, and urgency.

Repent—Believe—Follow

Why did the disciples tell this message? Not to gain a name for themselves. Not to satisfy curiosity about an unusual person who had made an impression on a handful of followers. Not merely to give an inspiring example. They told it with the hope and prayer that God would change men's lives, as their own lives had been changed by knowing Jesus and putting their trust in him.

So they never told it without pressing home to the conscience that men must do something—at once—about this message. They insisted that those who heard their story must make a decision. "Repent—" change your attitude; turn from evil; do not be a slave any longer to your own selfish will, but yield to God and let him have his way with you. "Believe—" accept the good news that God in Christ has offered redemption from the hold that evil has on you; put your trust in Christ as Redeemer and Lord; make him the center of your life and the commander of all your thoughts and words and deeds. "Follow—" walk in his ways; take up your cross in daily life; do God's will by the power of the Spirit, whom he gives to those who believe; tell others of what God has done for you through Christ and is ready to do for them in the same way; find your joy in this new faith and in the fellowship of those who share it with you; go forward in hope because you know that the future is safe with the God who has sent Christ to rescue you from what you are at present and to make you into the person you were meant to be.

This is the story that the followers of Jesus told. This is the message that gave them such earnestness and power. This is the gospel on which God founded the Church. It was in telling this vital story and in spreading the Christian faith and fellowship that the New Testament came to be written.

READING HINTS: To see what the early Christian preachers said, read some of the sermon summaries that The Acts gives. In doing so, look for the points we have noted in this chapter: fulfillment of God's promises to Israel, the power of God in the ministry of Jesus, the cross, the resurrection, the Lordship of Christ, the judgment to come, the call to repent and believe.

Begin with Acts 10: 34-43. It is brief and instructive. Then go on to read Acts 2: 14-36; 13: 16-41; 17: 22-31; 26: 1-23.

CHAPTER 2

How They Told the Story

EVEN the best story must be told well. The first Christians had a vital gospel to preach, but that alone does not explain why they persuaded so many people to listen. They also knew how to tell their story with skill. New listeners were fascinated, while those who already had heard the Christian teaching wanted to hear more of it. To understand the success of these preachers, we need to learn *how* they told the story. Then we need to know how they used it and applied it in their life together. As we come to understand this, we shall also begin to see why and how our four Gospels were written.

In Language People Understood

He who tells a story wants people to understand him. To get this result the speaker must talk in the hearer's own language. If only all people spoke the same tongue, this would raise no problem. But in the first century, as now, many different languages were in use. In Palestine, when Jesus and the apostles were teaching, two were widely used: Aramaic and Greek. Many Jewish scholars read Hebrew, in which almost all the Old Testament had been written, but the Jews no longer spoke it in daily life. Roman officials in Palestine may have used Latin in government documents, but seldom if ever in conversation; they spoke Greek.

Most widely used was Aramaic, which was closely akin to Hebrew. Even in our Gospels, written in Greek, we still find

Aramaic words and phrases. Mark, for example, reports that Jesus said: "Talitha cumi," "Little girl, arise" (Mark 5: 41); "Ephphatha," "Be opened" (Mark 7: 34); and "Abba," "Father" (Mark 14: 36). We learn from such expressions, and from the fact that "the great throng heard him gladly" (Mark 12: 37), that Jesus usually spoke in Aramaic. This was the language in which most of the earliest Christians talked. People spoke it not only in Palestine, but also in the neighboring regions of Phoenicia, Syria, and Mesopotamia.

But throughout the Roman Empire, Greek was the common language of most people. Though Latin was the native tongue of the Romans, the use of Greek had become common in all parts of the Roman world. The apostle Paul wrote his letters in Greek, even to the church in Rome. When the Roman church wrote to Corinth, about A.D. 96, they too wrote in Greek. Even in Palestine, Greek was the main language in at least a dozen cities. Then, too, more Jews lived outside of Palestine than in it, and most of those in foreign lands had learned to speak Greek. They had even translated their Hebrew Scriptures into Greek for use in reading and worship. The Christian Church took over this Greek translation, called the Septuagint, and New Testament preachers and writers used it wherever men spoke Greek.

Jesus himself no doubt spoke Greek a little. In Galilee, where both Gentiles and Jews lived, he must have been able to hear and learn that common tongue. And even when he taught in Aramaic, as he usually did, men who knew both Aramaic and Greek and heard him speak must often have gone away and told others in Greek what Jesus had said. Certainly the church at Jerusalem included from its first days disciples who could speak Greek. This we know from the sixth chapter of The Acts, which tells us that "Hellenists," or Greek-speaking Christians, were in the church there. We know it too from the fact that Barnabas, a member of this earliest church, could speak Greek; it was the language in which he later preached in the Roman world (Acts 4: 36; 11: 22; 13: 2).

So the gospel story was told from the first in at least two languages, Aramaic and Greek. Every year more Greek-speaking Christians were added to the Church, and by the time Paul's ministry ended the majority of Christians were people whose mother tongue was the widely used Greek language.

All the time, and in every place, the Christians preached the gospel in the language the people understood. And they talked in a way that all classes of people could follow. This is clear from the fact that from the beginning the great majority of the Church were ordinary people. The Christians were interested, not merely in well-educated and prominent persons, but in every man and woman and child. So they told their story in language that was clear and instructive to every attentive listener.

Not Written but Told

Today we receive much of our education from books, magazines, and newspapers. We often can read in the daily papers reports of meetings and speeches. Many people, while listening to a speech or lecture, take notes so that they will be able to remind themselves later what the speaker said.

The ancient Jews did not use such modern methods. They depended much more on memory of what they had heard. Men's minds were accustomed to attentive listening; keen memory held fast to what they heard speakers say.

For example, the Gospels tell us concerning the "tradition of the elders" (Mark 7: 5). This was the application of the Mosaic law which the Pharisees especially developed. They handed it down by word of mouth. Since the Jews had this practice of teaching the tradition in oral form, it did not occur to the hearers of Jesus to write down his words as he spoke them or to keep a diary of what he did. They remembered sayings and events and talked to others about them.

These oral reports of what God had done for men through Christ passed on from person to person. Were these reports accurate? Yes; we may be sure that in all essentials they were. The first listeners were keen of memory. Then, too, they knew that this was an important story; they therefore should tell it correctly. Besides, in the earliest days there were in many towns and cities of Palestine eyewitnesses who, because they had been with Jesus, could check on the accuracy of what other Christians taught. Concerning the public words and acts of Jesus many people were still alive who could tell what had happened; for other events the Twelve, or at least part of them, could tell whether the story was correct.

Told for a Purpose

Just how was the story handed on from person to person? Men did not always tell it in exactly the same form and order in which our Gospels now present it. The Church preserved this story because it had help to give to all who would listen and believe. The preachers and teachers told it to meet the needs of hearers and to promote Christian faith and living.

Remember that this was no ordinary biography that the Christians were telling. It was not a tale recounted merely to satisfy curiosity about an interesting man. It was rather a message about what God had done in Jesus Christ to save men from guilt and slavery to their own selfish wills, and to give them guidance and power for a life of obedience to God's will. This action of God fulfilled his earlier work and promise to Israel. It clearly made Jesus the central figure of history, and so the story concentrated on those elements which were explained in the first chapter—Christ's ministry, death, and resurrection, his present Lordship, and his future work of judgment and final redemption. Told to men guilty of wrongdoing, such a story called them to change the whole direction of their lives and to put their faith in the person who alone could bring about this change.

So the story was always told with an earnest practical purpose. This aim helped the Christians to remember the most important elements of the story of Christ and guided them in the way they told it. This does not mean that to make their preaching more interesting they felt free to change the story as they pleased. Quite the contrary. Because the story dealt with what God had done in Christ, they had to tell it faithfully. But they tried to present it effectively in order to win as many people as possible to believe the stirring gospel that set forth the real history, the actual teaching, and the present claim of Christ. They put this story in the way that would be as clear and winsome as possible.

In doing this, they did not always follow the actual order of events. We can understand this if we consider what a preacher does today. If he wishes to refer to a saying or event in the Gospels, he does not stop to tell all the things that precede or follow the passage he wants to use. He goes at once to the event or teaching that he can use to help his hearers. Nor does he always stop to say just when or where it happened. He may recall an incident that teaches a lesson about prayer, without telling what went before, what followed, where it happened, or when it took place. It happened; it can teach a modern congregation a vital truth to help them in their own faith and prayer; so he uses it for that purpose.

For the same reason the apostles and early teachers did not always give details about the place, time, and order of events and teachings. They told the story and taught the gospel in a way that met the immediate needs of their hearers. So when at a later time the Gospels were written, it was no longer possible to determine the exact time and place at which many events occurred. It was not possible; but it was not necessary, for the purpose of the Gospels is to promote faith in Jesus Christ and guide Christians in living. We are glad for every detail of place, time, and order that has been remembered, and we learn enough to give the needed outline of the career of Christ, but the other incidents and sayings are helpful to us even though we do not know when or where they took place.

The Use of the Story in Worship

The gospel story was used in many ways. One important use was in worship. When Christians gathered for worship, it was in the name of Christ; they were his disciples, who met under his Lordship and confessed their faith in him. In their prayers, they remembered what God had done for them in Christ, and recalled details of the gospel story as in gratitude they offered their petitions. In their sermons, the preacher recounted instructive events and sayings from Jesus' life, and spoke of them to his hearers. In their reading of their Scripture, our Old Testament, they recalled how God's promises written there came true in Christ.

Their attention, of course, was never directed merely toward the past; always they recalled the resurrection and the Lordship of Christ and his authority for the present and the future. At every service of worship the Christians remembered aspects of the life and work of Christ. Especially did they think of his death and resurrection. Again and again, at the common meals which the early Christians shared, they thought of the Last Supper, and so came to a deeper faith and understanding of Christ.

Preaching to Win New Converts

Why does the Church exist at all? Not simply for its own sake, as might be true of other organizations. It is here to serve Christ and win people to faith in him. It received from Christ himself the instruction to "be my witnesses . . . to the end of the earth" (Acts 1: 8). From the Day of Pentecost the Christians carried out their task, first in Jerusalem, and then in ever-expanding areas. In this preaching they constantly used the gospel story. They told how God had fulfilled his promise, saving them from what they were so that, in Christ, they might find a new destiny and meaning in life. They called men to believe in Christ and share the fellowship and work of the Church.

We are told how the Church grew as the result of this preaching. The Spirit of God used these preachers; the numbers grew from one hundred and twenty to three thousand, then to five thousand, to tens of thousands, and still more (Acts 1: 15; 2: 41; 4: 4; 21: 20). From community to community, at first in Jewish regions and population, and then among Gentile lands and peoples too, the Church spread. All this time the Christians were telling their story to others, frequently in places where large numbers were present, but often to one individual at a time. There were many preachers and witnesses, and they must have told the story in many ways. But it was always the same essential story, and they kept using concrete details about what Jesus did and said to illustrate and drive home the main points of the Christian gospel.

"Teaching Them . . . All Things"

It is not enough to tell people: Believe in Christ and take your place in the Church. They need to know what they are doing. That is why Christians used the gospel story in patient teaching of interested people who wanted to learn more about Jesus Christ and his claim. To such persons the teachers, of whom we read many times in the New Testament (for example, in Acts 13: 1; I Cor. 12: 28), not only told more details of the ministry and teaching of Jesus but also explained the meaning of what he had done and said. The earliest Christians were interested in winning as many as possible to Christian faith, but they did not want anyone to become a Christian unless he understood what it meant and was in earnest. So they kept teaching the stories and sayings of Jesus to make clear what the gospel message had to say and what it required.

Even after persons became Christians, they still needed to know more concerning Christ and his will for his followers. So the teachers also had to give members of the Church fuller instruction in the gospel story. The day could never come when the Church could stop teaching.

Light on the Problems of Living

New problems keep coming up in life. We can never solve them merely by rigid rules or by reports of what others have done. Nor do the problems of life end when a person becomes a Christian. He must face each new situation and choose his way by the help of God's Spirit. But for people perplexed about how to live their Christian life, there is no better guidance than in the things that Jesus said and did. So from the start of the Church wise leaders used the gospel material to give counsel to those who were facing difficult situations. Questions about prayer, the use of money, the attitude toward enemies, life in the home, and many other matters received light from the gospel story. Christians had not only God's Spirit to guide them but also the example and teaching of Jesus Christ to throw light upon their way.

In Defense of Christ and the Gospel

The early Christians preferred not to argue and debate. Their task was primarily to be witnesses. Now a witness is someone who talks, not about himself or his own opinions, but about someone else or about what has happened. He will, of course, be likely to convince others only if it is obvious that he himself is convinced of the truth of what he is saying. Thus the basic task of the first Christians was to tell the gospel story, to make it clear that they believed it, to tell what it had meant to them, and to urge others to believe in Christ.

But then as now opponents said many things against Jesus and the Christians. They ridiculed or denounced the new faith; they made false accusations concerning it and the disciples. Heated argument rarely wins others to accept the gospel, and to meet hate with hate would be to lose the Christian spirit. But it is possible to correct false statements and to defend the name of Christ from slanders. So the Christian leaders often had to use the gospel story in controversy; they often had to tell the truth about Christ so as to give a pointed answer to wrong statements that others were making.

This defense probably began with the Christian story of the cross. The Jewish leaders had rejected Jesus, and Pilate had crucified him on the pretense that he was a rebel and wrong-doer. So opponents could and did say that Jesus was clearly discredited and that therefore no one should respect or follow him. To answer this assertion the Church had to tell the story of the last days of Jesus' life in enough detail to show that he was not guilty of any wrongdoing, but had rather suffered a crying injustice. Christians also were quick to point out that in the resurrection God had reversed this mistake of men.

Other debates inevitably arose. For example, the Jews objected that Jesus often neglected or broke their ceremonial laws. So to justify the claim that Jews should follow Jesus, Christians had to repeat and defend his criticisms of the Jewish law and Sabbath observance. This was also the best way to justify the free attitude that the Christians took toward such Jewish practices. Thus, although controversy was not the main or usual method of the Christians, whose primary aim was to give their own positive witness to the gospel, they often had to defend the name and cause of Christ by answering slander and telling the story correctly.

The Need for a Written Record

The time soon came when the oral telling of the gospel could not by itself meet the needs of the Church. Every year the Church was spreading. The eyewitnesses were becoming fewer and fewer, while the total number of Christians steadily increased. Then, too, the Greek world was not so used to oral tradition as were the Jews. The large number of preachers and teachers needed something more permanent and definite to instruct them in the gospel story and to guide them in their work. Moreover, the very fact that the Old Testament had preserved in writing the earlier stages of God's redemptive work for men made it natural to record the most important event of all, God's work through Jesus Christ.

How soon did Christians begin to write down the story? We cannot say for certain. Luke tells us that before he wrote his Gospel many had undertaken to draw up a narrative about Jesus (Luke 1: 1). This suggests that not more than a generation after the death of Jesus men had begun to write down at least parts of the story. And this means that by about A.D. 50 men were putting down in writing the sayings of Jesus and the things that he did.

Writing Down the Story of Christ

Just what did the first written records contain? Perhaps one type of document simply copied out a selected series of Old Testament verses, such as we find quoted here and there in the Gospel of Matthew. These were passages that the Church saw had been fulfilled in Christ. It would have been convenient to have such a collection ready for frequent use.

Most probably someone had also made a collection of the teachings of Jesus. It gathered together the most important sayings and parables of Jesus for the use of teachers and leaders in the Church. The authors of our Gospels of Matthew and Luke, it appears, used such a collection. It is entirely possible that there were several small collections of this kind.

It may be that the written story of the arrest, trial, crucifixion, and resurrection was one early document. To defend Jesus against the false charge of being a rebel and wrongdoer, a connected story of his last days was needed. Note that over a quarter of each Gospel deals with the last week of Jesus' life. This careful account of how Jesus was unjustly put to death may have been written down even before Mark wrote.

But none of such early gospel records has survived. We have no written account earlier than the four Gospels that we now find in the New Testament. Back of Mark, which was the first of our four Gospels to be written, we may assume that there were other less complete documents and that our Gospel writers knew and used them. If so, they have not survived, because the Gospels that we know were fuller and more adequate. So the earlier writings soon fell into disuse, and because they were written on perishable writing materials, they disappeared. We do not need them. They would be most interesting to see; this we can tell from the few examples of ancient papyri found in Egypt with separate sayings of Jesus written on them. But we have what we need; the gospel story in our four Gospels preserves the story in a way that is adequate for our faith, our study, and our Christian living.

As we look back over the process by which, in more than one language and in many places, the story was preserved and retold and finally written down, one thing stands out: the interest of the Church in *the practical use* of the gospel story.

The Christians had a great interest in what Jesus said and did, because those facts helped them to see what God had done for them and what they therefore ought to do. The story was told orally, it was retold and preserved, it was written down first in part and then in a more complete record, because it was the one story that every person needed to know for his own faith and living. It was the gospel upon which the Church was founded and by which every Christian must find the answer to his needs. In it every hearer of the gospel can find the message of God and the hope of salvation; in it every believer must continually find the instruction and guidance he needs. The story was told, and the Gospels were finally written, by men of faith, to call others to faith and to build Christians up in the faith they had accepted.

Reading Hints: To see how the early Christians could have used the gospel story in their life and work, read the following passages and ask yourself how they would help the Church and the Christian:

In worship: Matt. 6: 1-18; I Cor. 11: 17-26. In preaching to win converts: Luke, ch. 15; John 1: 35-51. In teaching about Christ and Christian living: Mark 8: 27-38; Luke 10: 25-37. In debate with critics of Christ: Mark 2: 1 to 3: 6.

CHAPTER 3

The Gospel of Mark

A REWARD for good news; an offering for good news; good news—this is what the word for "gospel" had meant. But the Christians gave the old word a new meaning. To them it meant the good news that God had acted in Christ to save men, unite them in Christian fellowship, and give them power and hope (Mark 1: 15). They also used the word "gospel" more specifically to mean the story of the ministry, death, and resurrection of Jesus (Mark 1: 1). It was the story Christian leaders told of the historical career of Christ, in whom God had acted to carry out his purpose.

The time came when this story had to be written down to serve the needs of the Church. So the word "gospel" finally came to be used to mean the written record of the career of Christ, which was good news to every believer. This use of the word, so well known today, arose after the New Testament had been written.

Mark, the Earliest Complete Gospel

John Mark was the first to write such a Gospel. Most probably, even before Mark, others had written down reports of the teachings of Jesus. Possibly they also had written accounts of some things he had done. But, as far as we know, Mark's fuller account of Jesus' career was a new step in literary history. His originality in taking this step had great influence in the Church. When we study Matthew and Luke, the next Gospels to be written, we find that they are like Mark in many respects. They include almost all the events and sayings that Mark contains. Usually they give this material in the same order. To a great extent they tell it in the same Greek words. That is why these three Gospels are called the Synoptic Gospels; the word "synoptic" means "giving a common view" of the life and work of Christ. Of the three, Mark is the earliest; and by a literary method considered entirely proper in those days, the writers of Matthew and Luke appear to have made use of Mark as their main source.

By this extensive use of Mark they testify that to them it was a writing of great importance. They added much to what he had written, but they found his work too valuable to ignore. Obviously we do well to study Mark with care and interest.

Why Mark Was Well Fitted to Write

Why was John Mark the one who first wrote down in full and usable form the gospel story on which the Church's faith was based? His life had prepared him for this work. Son of Mary, an earnest Christian of Jerusalem in whose home the disciples met to worship, he knew well the leaders of the Church in its early days. The apostle Peter was one of those well known in Mark's home (Acts 12: 12). It has even been suggested, though it is not certain, that the young man who went to the Garden of Gethsemane to warn Jesus of his impending arrest was John Mark (Mark 14: 51, 52), and that Jesus' last supper with his disciples may have been held in John Mark's home.

John Mark also knew other well-known Christian leaders. He was the cousin of Barnabas (Col. 4: 10). When Barnabas and Paul went back to Antioch, after bringing a gift to the needy church at Jerusalem during a famine, they took Mark with them (Acts 12: 25). He went with them to Cyprus on their first missionary journey, but when they started into central Asia Minor, Mark turned back. His reason we do not know, but Paul thought Mark was a quitter (Acts 13: 5, 13) and refused to take him on the next journey. Barnabas, however, still believed in him, and took him on a second journey to Cyprus (Acts 15: 37-39).

A few important facts about Mark's later life are known. After some years, Paul spoke of Mark with approval. Clearly, Mark had made good and Paul was glad to recognize the fact (II Tim. 4: 11). Also, Peter, who had known Mark in Jerusalem, speaks of him as his "son" (I Peter 5: 13). This suggests that Peter had converted Mark to the Christian faith. It also indicates that Mark worked with Peter late in the latter's life.

Plainly, then, Mark had helped some of the greatest leaders of the Early Church. He had traveled widely, and knew the gospel story which the apostles preached. Indeed, he had had a part in teaching this message for many years. Who better could write down the gospel?

Written at Rome

The Gospel itself does not say who wrote it, nor does it state when, where, or why it was written. The headings and comments that some English Bibles give on these points were added much later. But the ancient and trustworthy tradition is that Mark wrote after Peter had been put to death in a persecution of the Christians at Rome by the emperor Nero. He saw the need for replacing the oral teaching of the apostles by a written record of what Jesus had done and said. This places the writing at Rome and dates it about A.D. 65 to 70.

This helps us to see his purpose. Mark was a Christian teacher. He was anxious to win as many as possible to the faith he held. He also wanted to instruct poorly informed Christians, and give all believers, especially the leaders, a written record to use in the work of the Church. Many could use such an account in private reading and study; all could use it in the meetings that Christians held for worship and teaching.

Mark knew that faith must be based on what God has done

for men in Jesus Christ, and that therefore men need a trustworthy record of the ministry and work of Christ. So he wrote down this gospel story which he had heard so often as he worked with the great leaders of the Church.

Not to Invent but to Report

In doing this work Mark's task was not to imagine material. This was not his personal story; it was the story on which the Church based its faith and life. Mark's duty was not to invent but to report. He had to show his skill, not by finding original things to say, but by presenting as clearly and helpfully as possible the story he had received. In this he certainly succeeded. The writers of the Gospels of Matthew and Luke thought so; they used almost everything that he included. The Christians who established the contents of the New Testament thought so too; they included Mark's Gospel in the Scripture.

To a large extent, at least, Mark depended on information furnished in word-of-mouth reports. Because he had lived and worked with great leaders, he knew what they taught. Indeed, an ancient Christian writer says that in his Gospel, Mark recorded the preaching of Peter. There is truth in this. Obviously he had heard in the teaching of the apostles most, if not all, of what he wrote down.

Possibly Mark also used written accounts of some parts of the story he had to tell. Some disputes that Jesus had with opponents we find grouped together in Mark 2: 1 to 3: 6; a group of parables are put together in Mark 4: 1-34; the end of the world is discussed in Mark, ch. 13; the unified story, in Mark 14: 1 to 16: 8, of the last days of Jesus' life is more detailed than the rest of the Gospel. It is possible, but by no means certain, that such passages had already been written down, and that Mark used the written form as a source. Even if this is so, it still is true that the main source of his information was the oral teaching of great Christian leaders he knew.

The Limits of His Story

Mark included in his story only the outline covered in the Church's public preaching. How far this outline went we may learn from Acts 1: 22 and 10: 34-43. These verses speak of the ministry of John the Baptist; then they tell of the baptism, ministry, death, and resurrection of Jesus. This is exactly the scope of Mark. Later writers, to satisfy the interest of the Church, told also something of the birth and infancy of Christ. But Mark kept his eye fixed steadily on the preaching message of the Church. Like the great preachers he knew, Mark told of the public ministry, the redeeming work, and the divine, victorious power of Christ. This was the story used to rouse men to faith. This was the story he told so well.

An early accident makes his story even briefer than it was at first. His Gospel as we now have it ends with Mark 16: 8. Ancient manuscript copies of Mark show this; Mark 16: 9-20 was added later. It is hard to think that Mark 16: 8 is a suitable ending for the Gospel. Did Mark fail to tell of the risen Christ's meeting with his disciples? He had promised to meet them (Mark 14: 28; 16: 7). We expect Mark to tell how they did see him. Then, too, the closing words of Mark 16: 8, "They said nothing to any one, for they were afraid," do not reflect the joy and glad confidence with which we expect the Gospel to end. So it is reasonable to conclude that Mark closed his story by telling how the risen Christ met his disciples in Galilee. At an early date this ending was lost, and someone added Mark 16: 9-20 to take its place.

The main fact remains clear. Mark began, as did the public preaching, with the ministry of John the Baptist and the baptism of Jesus, and ended with the resurrection.

A Vital Story Swiftly Told

What are the notable features of the Gospel of Mark? First of all, it tells a compact and effective story. It can be read easily in less than two hours. Each event is briefly told, each saying concisely reported. Many items are included, but each is put in few words.

Mark concentrates on important things. He does not stop to wonder what might have been. He spends little time on background, and usually leaves it to the reader to draw the lessons from his story. He pays scant attention to others besides Jesus, for Jesus is the central figure, and Mark mentions other people only as Jesus touches their lives.

The frequent "straightway" or "immediately" is a true clue to the steady movement of the story. Mark does not dally, nor stretch out his account. As soon as he has reported a concise teaching or swiftly described an incident, he goes right on to the next event.

The Essential Story in Clear Outline

The simple and clear outline is the second feature of Mark. When Jesus leaves the Jordan and the wilderness, after his baptism by John and the temptation (Mark 1: 1-13), he goes to his home region of Galilee. There, with Capernaum as his chief center, he carries on his ministry (Mark 1: 14 to 7: 23). When opposition becomes severe, he travels about more freely. But he never goes far beyond the borders of Galilee. His brief journeys into the neighboring regions of Phoenicia, Caesarea Philippi, and the Decapolis are times of withdrawal to teach the disciples, and he keeps returning to Galilee (Mark 7: 24 to 9: 50).

Finally, at the end of his ministry, he goes to Jerusalem to present his message and make his last appeal (Mark, ch. 10). Galilee was the scene of the public ministry as Mark tells it, but Jerusalem was the center of the religious life of the Jews, and there Jesus had to make the final appeal to his people and their leaders. The last third of the Gospel tells of the last week, and especially of the Last Supper, the arrest, trial, crucifixion, burial, and resurrection (Mark 11: 1 to 16: 8).

The Courage and Power of Jesus

Important to Mark, we note as a third feature, was the independence, courage, and power that Jesus showed in his ministry. He had no help from political or religious leaders. The former were indifferent or suspicious; the latter were jealous of their position and hostile to his message. He did his work with no official support; the power of God was at work in his ministry.

The common people were quick to notice this. They called him a prophet (Mark 8: 28). They realized that he spoke with authority and did not merely hand on older teaching, as did the interpreters of the Jewish law, the scribes (Mark 1: 22). In him they sensed divine prompting and power. They may not have understood him fully, but many believed that he was sent of God. His powerful word was matched by his powerful deeds. He healed the sick, and by his deeds of power he gave a clue that his authority came from God, who was at work in him.

His Chief Concern Was People

The constant concern of Jesus for human needs is a fourth emphasis of the Gospel of Mark. Jesus never centered his interest in Temple or sacrifices or Sabbath customs. He never put rules or traditions first. His interest was in people. To help one in need he was ready to break customs as to the Sabbath (Mark 2: 27) or disregard rules as to what was ceremonially clean or unclean (Mark 2: 16; 7: 1-23). With an unerring sense of what was important, he knew when to put aside usually helpful rules. In the place of traditions that cluttered up life he put active love (Mark 12: 28-34).

The Urgent Claim of Christ

Eagerness to make clear the supreme claim of Jesus Christ is the foremost of all features in this Gospel. Jesus calls men to follow him (e.g., Mark 1: 17, 20). He asks some men to give up their entire time to serve him and his cause. While he honors home and family, not even they are so important as the message he brings and the work he has to do (Mark 3: 31-35). Loyalty to God and Christ creates a new fellowship which takes first place, and whenever the choice has to be made Christ has first claim on life. Under him, every true loyalty can become a joy and a blessing, but no other loyalty can be allowed to rival or outrank this claim of Christ.

Hence the portrait of Jesus Christ is the most important thing in the Gospel. Mark writes as a Christian. He knows that the crowds thought of Jesus as a prophet, and that even Jesus once spoke of himself in that way (Mark 6: 4). But Mark also knows that this is not the whole story. He points to the unique role of Jesus by the use of four noteworthy titles.

The Son of God

First and foremost, Jesus is the "Son of God." This title probably stood in the opening sentence Mark wrote (Mark 1: 1), and the Voice at the baptism used it (Mark 1: 11). The climax of the Gospel's message about Jesus comes in Mark 15: 39, when the centurion, standing near the cross, declares, "Truly this man was God's Son."

This is Mark's firm faith. Jesus was indeed a true man, who knew the testing and trial of human life; he was the greatest man who ever lived. But he was more. Linked in close and unique relation with God, he was and is the Son of God. This faith Mark shared with other Christians, and it rested on words of Jesus himself (Mark 13: 32). As a faithful disciple, Mark could not say less of his Master.

The Son of Man

To express the truth about Jesus more fully, Mark uses three other titles current in the Church. He often quotes Jesus' favorite way of referring to himself: "The Son of man." Apart from Acts 7: 56, this title never appears in the New Testament except in the Gospels, where it always occurs in a saying that comes from Jesus.

What did the title mean to him? No doubt it included the truth that he shared the human lot, so that he hungered, suffered, and in general was subject to physical needs and human trials. But the title meant more than this to him. We find ancient Jewish writings that describe the Son of Man as a heavenly figure who acts for God. Jesus used the title in a similar way. He was not only to suffer for men by the will of God (Mark 10: 45); he was also to have a place of honor and praise with the Father, and was to return later to establish fully the Kingdom of God, which in his earthly ministry he had begun to establish (Mark 14: 62).

Thus with the thought of a lowly life, lived under the full stress of human need and suffering, the title "Son of Man" combines the further thought that God's Son who gives his life for men has honor with the Father, carries God's plan to victory, and will receive praise from all God's creatures.

The Christ of Israel

That Jesus was the Christ his disciples were slow to learn. Inspired by the Old Testament, Jews looked for a great leader, an "anointed one" (this is what the Hebrew word "Messiah" and the Greek word "Christ" both mean). God, they expected, would choose and equip and send him to be their deliverer and king. Usually they thought of him as an earthly king, who would be a wise and kindly guide to his people and a religious leader as well. He would free, rule, and guide them.

Because the Jews were looking for a leader to show power and authority more in the political than in the spiritual realm, they did not recognize in Jesus the promised Messiah. But the disciples, after living with him and learning from him, finally discerned that he was indeed the Messiah, and Peter spoke their conviction (Mark 8: 27-30). Jesus was God's chosen leader for his people.

Yet even the Twelve found it hard to understand the way that Christ chose. He did not try to win Israel by political and military means. He declared God's will; he announced that God was at work and that men should respond in faith; and against all odds he persisted in a ministry of unselfish good will and costly suffering. He spent much of his later ministry teaching his disciples that he must suffer for his people, to overcome evil and establish God's Kingdom. But not until after the resurrection did they really understand him and take up their work with power. Then Mark, like others, saw the truth. He presents Jesus as his people's Christ, who in his ministry and suffering fulfilled the deepest hopes of Israel, and so should receive the faith of Israel.

The Suffering Servant

But is suffering God's way to fulfill his purpose and help men? We all look instinctively for an easier, pleasant way. So did men in Jesus' day. Even his disciples found it hard to believe that "the Son of man must suffer" (Mark 8: 31). His opponents said bluntly that his crucifixion proved he was not from God. Yet, as Jesus tried to show his disciples, and as Mark reports so clearly, it was through this very way that the purpose of God would be done.

The Old Testament tells of the Servant of God who would suffer for God's people and so bless them. The outstanding passage that says this is Isa., ch. 53. From the failures and waverings of Israel, the prophet who wrote the latter part of The Book of Isaiah (chs. 40 to 66) drew the lesson God was teaching in history. Men are not saved by laws or even by good advice. They are helped by those who will live with people, suffer with and even for people, and unselfishly make every sacrifice to give help to others. The true members of Israel were to be such suffering servants of their fellows.

This truth found its unique fulfillment in Jesus himself. He saw that as the Son of Man and the Messiah of God's people, his way to bring them to God and to obedient life was the way of companionship, sympathy, and suffering for them. He, then, was the Suffering Servant, the perfect fulfillment and expression in life of the portrait that the prophet had painted. The triumph of Jesus comes by way of his suffering and humble service and death. The resurrection follows the cross.

Such is the figure of Jesus, as Mark has faithfully reported. Son of God, Son of Man, Christ—yes; but all these titles receive new meaning when coupled with the insight that Jesus is the Suffering Servant of God.

Jesus is not the Son of God *in spite of* his humble and suffering life. He does not have power and authority in spite of his human limitations and weakness. No; he is the true Son of the seeking Father of men *precisely because* he cares so much for men, precisely because he seeks at the greatest cost to win them for God and bring them to faith and obedience. He is the Son of the mighty Father precisely because his power to win men is the power of unselfish, sacrificing love.

Jesus did not apologize, Mark does not apologize, the grateful Christian does not apologize, for the cross. Christ is not honored even though he was crucified. He is honored and triumphant precisely because he loyally went to the cross and accepted the full measure of suffering in order to do God's will and redeem men (Mark 10: 45).

READING HINTS: This Gospel is no longer than many short stories in modern magazines. Mark wrote it without any chapter and verse divisions. (The chapter divisions date from 1228; our verse divisions from 1551.) He meant it to be read as one story. Read it without stopping if you can. It is worth it.

Note that Jesus preaches about the Kingdom of God: Mark 1: 14, 15; 4: 1-34.

Note also how the story leads up to the cross, and calls the disciple to follow the same path: Mark 3: 6; 8: 27-38; 9: 30-41; 10: 32-45.

Great Verses to Think About: Mark 1: 38; 2: 17; 2: 27, 28; 8: 34; 9: 35; 10: 45; 11: 25. Underline in your own Bible the verses that help you most.

CHAPTER 4

The Gospel of Matthew

TODAY the great majority of Christians are Gentiles. Though the Church includes many Jews, they are a very small part of the Christian group. Probably not one in a hundred present-day disciples of Jesus is of Jewish origin. How different it was in the beginning! Jesus himself was a Jew. So were all his first disciples. The basic background of Jesus and his followers was Judaism.

It is well that the Gospel of Matthew stands first in our New Testament to recall these Old Testament roots and Jewish ties of our faith. The writer of this Gospel is himself a Jewish Christian, and he is eager to recall the greatness of God's gifts to his chosen people Israel. No one but such a Jewish Christian could have written this Gospel. He emphasizes the Jewish setting of the gospel story. He shows a strong concern to lead his fellow Jews to believe in Christ.

A Gospel for the Jews

At the very beginning of the Gospel stands a genealogy, that is, a list of the ancestors of Jesus (Matt. 1: 1-17). To us this may seem a most uninteresting way to start a story. But the writer has a purpose in tracing the family history. The family tree shows that Jesus was not only a Jew, but was also of royal descent. His ancestry could be traced to King David and the honored forefather Abraham.

With such an ancestry, Jesus was fitted for his unique place in the history of this people. As the Son of David he was the rightful "king of the Jews" (Matt. 2: 2; 27: 37). The other Gospels include this fact, but the writer of Matthew emphasizes it. He does so to say to the Jews that they should put their faith in Jesus as the one who fulfills God's promises to them.

That Jesus fulfilled Israel's hopes the author stresses in many ways. He frequently cites Old Testament passages to show how the coming and ministry of Jesus carried out the promises of the Jewish Scriptures (e.g., Matt. 3: 3). The Gospel fulfills the Old Testament; Jesus came not "to abolish the law and the prophets; . . . but to fulfill them" (Matt. 5: 17). The Jew who found the Word of God in his Scriptures should therefore put his faith in Jesus as the one to whom the Scriptures point.

This Gospel further emphasizes that Jesus deliberately directed his ministry to Israel alone. He devoted himself to his own land and his own people. Only rarely and briefly did he step across the borders of his native land. Even then, when the appeal came to help a Gentile woman who wanted him to heal her daughter, he hesitated; he declared that by God's plan he must concentrate his efforts on his own people: "I was sent only to the lost sheep of the house of Israel" (Matt. 15: 24). In sending out the Twelve, all of whom were Jews, he instructed them to go to their fellow countrymen: "Go nowhere among the Gentiles, and enter no town of the Samaritans, but go rather to the lost sheep of the house of Israel" (Matt. 10: 5, 6). Only twice does he heal a Gentile, both times after special appeal and then only at a distance. All this should make Jewish readers see that Jesus came to them first of all, and that they therefore should put their trust in him and live as his disciples.

A Faith for All Men

But the purpose of God looked beyond Israel, and the Christian writer of the Gospel of Matthew says so. While Jesus limited his ministry almost entirely to his own people, this was for reasons of strategy. There was the place to begin, with the people whom God had chosen and to whom he had given the Scriptures and the prophets. But Jesus came to Israel to prepare for the wider spread of the gospel through Israel.

The Wise Men from the East were Gentiles. In their coming to Jesus (Matt. 2: 1) the writer sees an early hint that the birth of Jesus was to benefit the entire world, Gentiles as well as Jews. Then, too, mere physical descent is not enough. To the Jew descended from Abraham salvation is offered first, but this does not guarantee divine blessing. Faith and obedience to God are basic. Therefore Jesus, like John the Baptist before him (Matt. 3: 7-10), declares that unbelieving Jews will suffer ruin, and obedient Gentiles from all regions will receive blessings in the Kingdom of Heaven (Matt. 8: 11, 12). The risen Christ directs his apostles to carry the gospel story to "all nations" (Matt. 28: 19), and to baptize and receive into the fellowship of the Church all who believe.

A faith for all the world must have one common center. The bond of this new fellowship could no longer be the Promised Land of Palestine, or the Holy City Jerusalem. Neither could it be the Temple, or the synagogue, or the tie of race, or the authority of priests and rabbis. The new center was the person of Jesus himself. When he called men to follow him, he took the first step in forming this new fellowship. It was not yet clear to his followers that this group was to include men of all nations, but it was already plain that the center and authority of the group was Jesus their Master.

A little later Jesus selected twelve followers to take special responsibility (Matt. 10: 2-4). Even then it was not clear that this would lead to a world Church; the twelve apostles reminded men of the twelve tribes of Israel. But the basic thing in their life and work was their central loyalty to Christ. If Judaism refused to follow him. the leaders of a new religious fellowship were ready in the Twelve.

The same possibility of a break with the officials of Judaism was present when Peter and the rest of the Twelve recognized in Jesus the expected Messiah of the Jews (Matt. 16: 16). The Messiah was expected to lead the Jews; indeed, he was to be the supreme authority for every true Jew. But he was also to rule all the nations. If other leaders in Israel refused to accept and follow him, those who did believe in him had to put him first. They had to break with hostile Jewish officials and live as a Christ-centered fellowship with a task in the entire world.

Many things were not clear at first for the disciples. But they knew that Jesus as the Christ was their supreme authority, and that he was the world figure whom they must serve.

Christ and His Church

What did Jesus say about the Church? He said surprisingly little. The only Gospel that contains the word "church" is the Gospel of Matthew, and it has the word in but two passages (Matt. 16: 18; 18: 17). Why? Because Jesus concentrated to the end of his life on his efforts to reach and win his people. He spoke to them of the Kingdom of Heaven, or the Kingdom of God, which means the same thing; he taught God's chosen people the will of God; he challenged them to see that God was at work in their midst and that they should accept him as their God-sent leader. He spent no time in organizing a Church separate from the religious life of the chosen people. He must first offer Israel the opportunity to be the nucleus around which the world Church would be built.

But evidently to his followers he did on rare occasions speak concerning his Church, the fellowship of his followers. This Church is to do all it can to reconcile disciples who are at odds (Matt. 18: 17); it is to act in discipline only as a last resort. More important, it is based upon the faith in Jesus as "the Christ, the Son of the living God" (Matt. 16: 16), the faith of which Peter was the original spokesman.

From both the Gospels and the book of The Acts it is clear

that Peter was the active spokesman and leader of the Twelve. Jesus expected him to exercise real leadership and to teach with vigor and authority. This, of course, does not mean that Jesus designated Peter as the first pope. For one thing, he says nothing of any successors to Peter; he establishes no priestly system. In the second place, none of the other Gospels mentions the Church or the teaching authority of Peter, and the book of The Acts and the Epistles show no sign that the other apostles regarded Peter as the one supreme ruler of the Church. On the contrary, at the conference at Jerusalem (Acts, ch. 15), it is not Peter but James the Lord's brother who presides; and at Antioch, when Peter acts in a wobbly and narrow manner, Paul bluntly rebukes him (Gal. 2: 11-21). Plainly the Early Church did not teach that the important role Peter received from Jesus gave him also complete supremacy and absolute authority.

Even in the Gospel of Matthew, Jesus gives to the other disciples (Matt. 18: 18) the same power to teach and administer the affairs of the Church that in Matt. 16: 19 he gives to Peter. Indeed, he promises that any two or three, when fully loyal to him, may pray to the Father and receive the request they make (Matt. 18: 19).

Peter was a great disciple and leader. We owe him gratitude for taking the leading role in the earliest days. But not even in the Gospel of Matthew does Jesus say anything about an all-powerful priesthood that can take away from other disciples their voice in the direction of the Church. Jesus expected his followers to be bound together by their common faith in him. This, he knew, would lead to a separate fellowship if official Judaism did not accept his leadership and put its faith in him. In his group there would be leaders, and the Twelve and especially Peter would have important work to do and strong influence to exercise. The writer of the Gospel of Matthew saw that Jesus had thus laid the basis of the Apostolic Church in which he lived, and he writes as a member of that Church and with a vision of the world mission that was opening out before it.

Teaching Arranged by Topics

The writer of the Gospel of Matthew knows that the Church, to be truly Christian, must remember and understand what Jesus said. So he includes much more of Jesus' teaching than does Mark. And he is careful to arrange his material in as useful an order as possible. He was not the first to have this interest. Jesus himself taught in a simple, clear, and forceful way. But this writer uses every skill to arrange the teaching so that it will be both clear and easily remembered.

One way in which he helps the reader is by groupings of threes, fives, and sevens. In Matt. 6: 1-18, for instance, occur three examples of ways in which one should avoid outward parade in religious life; they deal with almsgiving, prayer, and fasting. So, too, there are three temptations of Jesus (Matt. 4: 1-11), three prayers in Gethsemane (Matt. 26: 39-44), and three denials by Peter (Matt. 26: 69-75).

There are five great discourses in which most of the teaching of Jesus is gathered: the Sermon on the Mount (Matt., chs. 5 to 7), the Charge to the Twelve Apostles (Matt., ch. 10), the Parables Concerning the Kingdom (Matt., ch. 13), the Teaching Concerning Greatness and Forgiveness (Matt., ch. 18), and the Teaching Concerning the End of This Age (Matt., chs. 24; 25). There are seven parables in Matt., ch. 13, and seven woes against the scribes and Pharisees in Matt., ch. 23. Such arrangement of teaching in groups helps the reader to understand and remember what Jesus said.

The writer groups these sayings according to the subject that they discuss rather than according to the time when they were spoken. For some teaching he gives the original occasion, but his real interest is to group together in a convenient way the teaching of Jesus on a subject.

An example is Matt. 5: 17-48. Here we find a series of points on the relation between the teaching of Jesus and that of the Old Testament. Did Jesus say all these things at one time? The Gospel of Luke has parallels to some of them, but it has such parallels in more than one place. The Gospel of Matthew, then, gathers together, according to topic, passages not grouped together in the tradition as Luke knew it. Such topical arrangement is particularly noticeable in the Gospel of Matthew. This is for convenience in teaching and learning. It shows the mind of a teacher in the writer of the Gospel.

The Gospel Not a Code of Laws

To group the teachings of Jesus in such orderly form makes it sound a bit like a set of rules. It sounds a little as though Jesus had given a series of classified laws about how man must live. Indeed, some students of this Gospel have actually thought that its writer meant to present the teaching of Jesus as a new law, better than the law of Moses and therefore binding upon all. They have suggested that the five great discourses are made important in this Gospel so that the alert reader will notice them, and see that the five books of Moses must now yield first place to this new statement of the law of God, given through Jesus in his teaching.

This idea is false. Even in this Gospel there is much teaching of Jesus outside of the five great discourses. In these discourses the material is grouped, not to give a law, but to aid teaching and learning. If we look at this teaching, we see at once that we cannot take it as a law. Jesus called for repentance and faith; these depend on the heart and will, and laws cannot control them. He appealed for love of God and neighbor; love comes from the heart, and finds expression not by rule, but as each new occasion requires. Jesus himself discarded rules and customs when they hindered true faith and friendly living; he expected his followers to do the same.

The orderly arrangement of teaching in the Gospel of Matthew helps us to learn the message of Jesus. It must not make us think of Jesus as a lawmaker who tried to control life by rigid external rules.

Sources of Information

Where did the writer of the Gospel get his material? He was a teacher in the Church, and what he writes down was not new to him. Some of what he writes he may have heard from eyewitnesses and teachers of the gospel story. But when we compare the Gospel of Matthew with the Gospels of Mark and Luke, and note how they agree in material, order, and Greek wording, it becomes almost certain that back of this Gospel are written Greek sources. The basic one was the Gospel of Mark, most of which is used in Matthew, although usually in shortened form. In addition to Mark, there probably was another written source; it contained mostly teachings of Jesus and was used by the writers of both Matthew and Luke. Perhaps the writer of Matthew also quoted from a collection of "testimonies," giving Old Testament passages that the Christians saw had been fulfilled in the life and ministry of Christ. The genealogy in Matt., ch. 1, and indeed the entire infancy story in the first two chapters, may have come to the writer in written form.

Back of this Gospel, then, were at least two written sources: Mark and a collection of Jesus' teachings. And the writer may have used other shorter documents. Further, the writer no doubt drew upon still other gospel traditions which came to him by word of mouth.

The Writer a Jewish Christian Teacher

Who wrote the Gospel of Matthew? In Christian tradition, the author is said to be Matthew, one of the Twelve, who had been a tax collector before he left his business to follow Jesus (Matt. 9: 9). No other name has ever been suggested for the author. So it is reasonable to conclude that Matthew had some connection with its writing. However, its author used the

Gospel of Mark, who was not an apostle but who depended on Peter and others for information. This is not what we would expect the writer of Matthew to do if he were himself an apostle. Why would he have used as his basic source a writing by one who had not been a companion of Jesus?

An ancient tradition suggests a convincing solution of the difficulty. The oldest report about the author comes from Papias, in the middle of the second century. He says that "Matthew collected the *logia* (sayings, or oracles) in the Hebrew [or Aramaic] language, and each one interpreted them as he was able." This may mean that Matthew gathered together a collection of Old Testament passages such as the writer of our Gospel quotes so often. Or, more likely, Matthew may have written down the collection of the teachings of Jesus ("sayings") that the writers of the Gospels of Matthew and Luke used as a source. This would explain how the name of Matthew became connected with the Gospel; its writer had used a source that Matthew composed. The name, then, of the final writer of the "Gospel of Matthew" is not known; he was a brilliant and loyal Jewish Christian teacher.

When was the Gospel completed? Since none of the Gospels says when it was written, we cannot give an exact date. The one clear conclusion is that, since its author used Mark, the Gospel of Matthew was written later than that of Mark. This suggests a date later than A.D. 70, perhaps in the 80's or even about A.D. 90.

Jesus the Jew

The gospel the writer tells is not his own personal story. It is the gospel about Jesus Christ. It is the story that is the basis and message of the Church. So the author uses all his skill to make clear the divine mission of Jesus Christ and his urgent claim on the Jews and all men. What stands out in this portrait of Christ?

Great emphasis is laid on the fact that Jesus was a Jew.

That he came as a Jew and addressed himself to Jews is emphasized in many ways: by the genealogy that traces his ancestry back through the line of Jewish kings to the Jewish forefather Abraham; by the geography that shows that the scene of the story was limited almost entirely to Palestine; by the frequent use of the Jewish Scripture; by the gathering of the Twelve, who all were Jews; by the persistent and explicit limiting of the ministry of Jesus to Jews. He accepted the Jewish Scripture as his Scripture; his work was not "to abolish . . . but to fulfill" what that Scripture said (Matt. 5: 17). He carried forward to its climax what God had done for Israel. This Jewishness of Jesus is clear in all the Gospels, but here it is strongly emphasized in order to make a powerful appeal to Jews to believe in Christ.

Jesus the Jewish Messiah

To the writer of Matthew it is particularly important that Jesus is the Jewish Messiah. He is "the son of David" (Matt. 1: 1; 21: 9); he is the "king of the Jews" (Matt. 2: 2; 27: 37). Every Jew therefore should give him trust and obedience. The writer believes that Jesus is "the Son of God"; indeed, he reports that this title was part of the full Messianic title of Jesus that Peter used at Caesarea Philippi (Matt. 16: 16). He also reports often that Jesus spoke of himself as "the Son of man," serving now in a humble way, but destined by his suffering to save men and to triumph by the power and purpose of God. Thus, like Mark, he presents Christ as the Suffering Servant of whom the writer of Isa., ch. 53, spoke.

But the writer of Matthew puts a special emphasis on the fact that Jesus fulfills the hope of Israel—the long-cherished hope that God would send a chosen descendant of David to deliver and rule and guide his people. Jesus is that "Son of David." He is the rightful King of Israel. Israel therefore should become his disciples; rulers and common people alike should rejoice to be his followers.

Jesus the Supreme Teacher

The teaching skill of Jesus has never been questioned. Men have rightly called him "the master teacher." He spoke with authority and taught with power. This Gospel gathers together in orderly form his most important teaching and it is among the greatest possessions of mankind. It is important not merely because it is brilliant, but because it is true, because it deals clearly and effectively with the most vital subject, man's life before God. It reveals God's work and will; it lays bare man's nature, his needs, his relation to God, and his duties.

Such matchless teaching is the more important to the writer of this Gospel because it comes not merely from some good and capable teacher, but because it is the word of the Supreme Teacher, the Christ, the Lord of his people, the one who is to judge the world. Because he believes that true life both in this world and in that which is to come depends on the right relation to God through Christ, the Gospel author uses every effort to make clear what Jesus taught.

Jesus Both Friendly and Stern

Does it make any difference what men do about Christ? Men have sometimes spoken of Jesus as a meek and gentle man, as though he would never condemn any person. It certainly is true that in the Gospel of Matthew, as in the other Gospels, Jesus shows strong sympathy with all in need; he was particularly sympathetic with those in pain or sorrow or want. He was always ready with a word of forgiveness and hope for anyone ready to change his attitudes and give up evil ways.

But Jesus never told men it made no difference to God how they lived. On the contrary, he denounced those who with calloused consciences continued to do wrong or treated their fellows without mercy (Matt. 18: 21-35; 23: 23-28). He condemned those who made religion a mere outward form, or who used it for personal benefit or to feed their pride (Matt. 6: 1-18). He warned that to hear and reject his message would bring certain disaster (Matt. 7: 26, 27).

The Gospel of Matthew contains more warnings of divine judgment on evil, more stern references to the sad fate of those who deliberately reject the claim of Christ, than does any other Gospel. While all four Gospels share this view, this one underlines it. The writer intends to make the reader see how crucial is the choice between faith and unbelief. The man who rejects Christ is headed for tragedy, not because Christ refuses to help him, but because man's decision concerning the claim of Christ determines his direction and shapes his future. He who stubbornly refuses to accept the help that God sends in Christ shuts the door against himself and loses the privilege that the gospel so freely offers.

Reading Hints: Read the entire Gospel. Pay special attention to the five great collections of the teaching of Jesus: The Sermon on the Mount (Matt., chs. 5 to 7), The Charge to the Twelve Apostles (Matt., ch. 10), The Parables Concerning the Kingdom (Matt., ch. 13), The Teaching Concerning Greatness and Forgiveness (Matt., ch. 18), and The Teaching Concerning the End of This Age (Matt., chs. 24; 25).

CHAPTER 5

The Gospel of Luke

WHY did the Church put twenty-seven books in the New Testament? Why not stop with four Gospels? Jesus is the central figure of the entire New Testament and to him it directs all Christian faith and thinking. What God did for men through Jesus Christ is the heart of the Christian message. The Gospels tell the basic story on which the Christian faith and Church are founded. Yet the Church was led by God to add other writings. It added The Acts, for example. Why?

More Had to Be Told

All four of the Gospels point ahead. None of the Gospel writers thought that he had told the entire story. Each one ends his account with a clear witness to the resurrection of Jesus, and the resurrection means that Jesus is the living Christ and the active Lord of his Church. Thus each Gospel points ahead to the further work of Christ and to the ongoing work of God. That story also had to be told. The later Church needed to know how Christ sent the Holy Spirit and how the Holy Spirit gave power and guidance to the disciples as they founded the Church and spread the gospel.

Then, too, we need to remember that it was these disciples who gave us the gospel story itself. To understand the work of Christ we need to see his career as a whole. This was possible only after the death and resurrection of Jesus. Only then could the Church tell the full gospel story. After God raised Christ from the dead and gave the Holy Spirit to the Church, those who had been with Jesus began to give the full and basic testimony on which the faith of the Church would always be founded.

Plainly, therefore, the work of the preachers and teachers in the apostolic age was immensely important. It was then that the Church took form, the gospel story was told in full, and the Gospels were written. The account of how God founded the Church by the Spirit-guided witness and work of Christ's disciples is an essential part of the Christian message.

But the Gospels do not tell the story of this later period. From them we learn something of the faith and teaching of the apostolic age, but their purpose is to tell clearly the central story of the ministry and work of Jesus. They point ahead, but they do not carry the story beyond the resurrection.

One man saw the need and met it. He continued the gospel narrative to include the story of what the disciples later did. He put into one story both the work of Jesus and the later ministry of his disciples. Today we have his writing in a separated form; the Gospel of Luke we find among the Gospels, but the second part, The Acts, which gives the story of the apostolic age, comes later to prepare the way for the letters that then follow. This is a convenient arrangement, but we must see what the original writer did. In one work, which we may call Luke-Acts to indicate its unity, he told the one connected story.

He wrote one work in two parts. Even today, an author may publish a long work in two volumes. In ancient times, when writing materials were fragile, an author divided a writing of some length into two or more parts or books. The first part he opened with a general preface; in it he stated his purpose. Then in the second part, and in as many other parts as followed, he first referred briefly to what he had already written and quickly turned to the next stage of his story. This is exactly what we find in Luke-Acts. The Gospel begins with a literary preface that states the reason for writing and what is to be told (Luke 1: 1-4); the book of The Acts first recalls what the Gospel had told (Acts 1: 1) and then continues the story.

"Luke the Beloved Physician"

Luke was the man who wrote this two-part work. The writing itself does not say this. It was not usual for a writer of a narrative to tell his name. (The headings of the books in our English Bibles were not part of the original writings.) But Luke-Acts shows literary interest and ability; it opens with a formal literary preface (Luke 1: 1-4); the name of the writer must have been known from the day it was published. The earliest tradition names Luke as the author, and no other name has ever been suggested. "Luke the beloved physician" (Col. 4: 14), companion of Paul on his missionary journeys, was the writer of Luke-Acts.

Luke had been with Paul more than once on the apostle's journeys. This fact we find clearly indicated in The Acts, where in four passages Luke uses "we" to indicate that he too was present with Paul (Acts 16: 10-17; 20: 5-15; 21: 1-18; 27: 1 to 28: 16). He was with Paul during at least two imprisonments, the one in which Paul wrote Colossians (Col. 4: 14) and Philemon (Philemon 24), and the one in which he wrote the statement of II Tim. 4: 11 that "Luke alone is with me."

It is often said that a physician must have written Luke-Acts. The language, many argue, is that of a medical man. The evidence does not compel this conclusion, but goes well with it. Taken together, Christian tradition and the language of the writing make it clear that "Luke the beloved physician" (Col. 4: 14), a companion of Paul and a Gentile Christian, wrote this fuller form of the gospel story.

He is the only Gospel writer who tells us anything about the situation in which he writes. The other Gospels concentrate wholly on the story they have to tell. Their authors seek no literary credit, for they know that the story they tell is not their own but is rather the Church's possession. Even Luke is far more interested in the gospel than in literary credit. But he comes to his task with a background of Gentile culture which the other Gospel writers do not have, and by beginning with a literary preface (Luke 1: 1-4) he tells us much about how he came to write.

How Luke Learned the Story

Luke had not been a companion of Jesus. He could not speak as an eyewitness; his purpose was to tell clearly, accurately, and in order the story that eyewitnesses had delivered to the Church. Nor was Luke a leading minister or preacher. Preachers with whom he had lived had told him what the eyewitnesses said. Furthermore, Luke states plainly that he was not the first to write down the gospel story. He sets out to write a fuller story, extending from the birth of John the Baptist and Jesus to the end of Paul's career. But many before him had written an account of the work of Jesus. He knows their writings, and in accord with the literary practices of that time, he uses them as far as they help him.

But Luke is not limited to the written records he knows. He had been present at many important events. Then, too, while with Paul, he had heard the apostle tell many things about Christ and the gospel and the earliest days of the Church. He had heard other teachers assist Paul by instructing inquirers and believers in the essentials of the Christian story. When Paul went to Jerusalem for the last time (Acts 21: 17), Luke went with him, and was with him, it appears, during the two years Paul was a prisoner at Caesarea in Palestine (Acts 24: 27). These years in Palestine gave him opportunity to talk with many Christians, some of whom had no doubt seen and heard Jesus, and many of whom could tell of the first days of the Church. It is not surprising that Luke felt prepared to write an orderly and accurate account. His background suggests that he could write a dependable history.

Nor is it surprising that Luke used the Gospel of Mark as one of his sources. He knew Mark; twice we hear that Luke and Mark were both with Paul (Col. 4: 10, 14; II Tim. 4: 11). He knew too the collection of Jesus' teaching that the writer of Matthew also used, which the apostle Matthew may well have written. He had other sources of information, some of them no doubt discovered during his stay in Palestine. These included some of the famous parables and stories that Luke alone gives us. In addition, he was told the story of the birth and childhood of John the Baptist, which no other Gospel contains. He also learned a beautiful story of the birth and early years of Jesus himself. These narratives were too valuable to omit.

So Luke used sources, written and oral, but the result is his own work. One scholar has called his Gospel "the most beautiful book ever written." In Christian faith and with great skill he combined what he had learned into a strong and priceless story. It told of God's work to redeem men and build the Church through Christ and the Holy Spirit.

When Did Luke Write?

When did Luke write? Since he used the Gospel of Mark as one source for his Gospel, he obviously wrote after Mark did. If we date Mark between A.D. 65 and 70, then Luke-Acts belongs several years later, perhaps sometime during the 80's.

One can argue for an earlier dating. The book of The Acts ends with Paul in prison at Rome. It does not tell what happened to Paul after the closing two years of the story (Acts 28: 30). Why did Luke stop his story there? We want to know whether Paul did any further work and when his life ended. Could it be that Luke wrote before the trial of Paul took place, and so could tell no more than he did? If that were true, the date of The Acts would be about A.D. 63, and the date of the Gospel of Luke would be shortly before that time.

The chief difficulty with this view is that it would make us date Mark, which Luke used as a source, back in the 50's. This is contrary to the earliest tradition that Mark was written after the death of Peter, and so not before the late 60's. For this reason the date in the 80's is preferable for Luke-Acts.

"All Flesh Shall See the Salvation of God"

Luke, like the other Gospel writers, writes as a believer. His real concern was not to win a great reputation as an author. He wanted to help the Church and spread the Christian faith. To be sure, he addresses Theophilus in the preface. This man was probably a well-to-do Gentile Christian; perhaps he was a Roman official of some importance. But the purpose of Luke was not simply to please or help one individual, however important his position. It was to provide a record that would be useful in the worship and life of the Church and in the hands of its teachers. He wrote as a Christian to serve the cause of Christ.

How far does Luke, the only Gentile among the Gospel writers, see the ties that bind the Christian faith with the Old Testament and Israel? He sees them clearly. He quotes the Old Testament as Scripture. He reports frankly that Jesus' ministry was among the Jews. Had he known of a ministry to Gentiles, it would have delighted him to tell of it. But he knew that Jesus, to lay the foundations of the Church, deliberately confined his ministry to his own people. In the infancy narratives he gives a beautiful picture of the life of devout first century Jews. Famous hymns of faith, in the language and spirit of the Scriptures of Israel, occur only in Luke's Gospel: the Magnificat (Luke 1: 46-55), the Benedictus (Luke 1: 68-79), the Gloria in Excelsis (Luke 2: 14), and the Nunc Dimittis (Luke 2: 29-32). (These hymns are known by the first words in their Latin version.)

But coupled with this deep appreciation of the Jewish setting of the gospel story is a steady series of hints that the gospel is for all men. Jesus is a "light for revelation to the Gentiles" as well as "for glory to thy people Israel" (Luke 2: 32). In quoting Isaiah concerning John the Baptist, Luke goes on farther than the other Gospels, until he reaches the ancient promise that "all flesh shall see the salvation of God" (Luke 3: 6). He traces the genealogy of Jesus not simply to the Jewish ancestors David and Abraham, as is done in Matthew, but to Adam, the forefather of all mankind (Luke 3: 38). Jesus sends out not only the Twelve, who went to Israel (Luke 9: 1-6), but also the Seventy; this seems to suggest that the gospel is for all mankind, which in ancient tradition was divided into seventy nations (Luke 10: 1). Favorable references to Samaritans, found only in this Gospel, also suggest that the faith should include other than Jews (Luke 10: 33; 17: 15 f.). The gospel of Christ is for all men, as Luke goes on to show in The Acts.

Jesus was a world figure. Luke the Gentile had a keen sense of this fact. Many people undoubtedly thought the career of Jesus an unimportant happening among unimportant people in an out-of-the-way place. Luke insists that "this was not done in a corner" (Acts 26: 26). By the way he dates the opening events of his story he means to say that here is a narrative of world importance. He not only tells that Herod was king of Judea at the start of the infancy story (Luke 1: 5). He also refers to the decree of Caesar Augustus (Luke 2: 1). In particular, he names both local and world rulers to date the opening of John the Baptist's ministry (Luke 3: 1 f.). This he does to say that the gospel story is of epoch-making importance. The world and its rulers cannot ignore the coming and work of this Jesus. For a time they tried to do so, but Luke has long since been proved to be right.

Special Features in Luke

Nearly half of what we find in Luke occurs in no other Gospel. Among this new material are the infancy narratives and many stories, sayings, and parables. Much of what is new

Luke gives in the long story of the journey of Jesus to Jerusalem (Luke 9: 51 to 19: 27). In this travel narrative Luke groups many new items that seemed to fit there best. Whenever possible, he gives a definite historical setting for each saying and event, but in some cases the people who told him the story, or the source he used, did not know just when or where an event occurred or a saying was spoken.

Luke's main interest is not in the order of events but in the teaching of Jesus and in the Master's work for men. Six aspects of that work receive special emphasis in this Gospel.

1. The role of women is more prominent in this Gospel than in any other. The birth and infancy narratives are told from the point of view of the women Mary, Elizabeth, and Anna. Only Luke tells of the group of women who helped Jesus in his work and supplied the needs of the traveling disciples (Luke 8: 1-3). He tells of the widow of Nain (Luke 7: 11, 12), the sinful woman who was sorry for her sin and was assured of forgiveness by Jesus (Luke 7: 36-50), the sisters Mary and Martha (Luke 10: 38-42), and the women who sorrowed when Jesus was taken to the cross (Luke 23: 27). Only Luke reports the parable of the woman who searched for the lost coin, as Jesus seeks "lost" people (Luke 15: 8-10). Only in Luke do we find the parable of the widow who pestered the unjust judge until he gave her justice (Luke 18: 1-8). Jesus' understanding of women and sympathy with their needs deeply impressed Luke.

2. The concern of Jesus for the poor stands out in this Gospel. Luke includes on this point stories and sayings that other Gospels also give. But in addition he reports important teaching that we find nowhere else. He gives a form of the Beatitudes and Woes that defends and befriends the poor (Luke 6: 20-26). In such parables as those of the Rich Fool (Luke 12: 16-20) and the Rich Man and the Beggar Lazarus (Luke 16: 19-31), Jesus shows how possessions can dominate and distort a man's life; he warns and denounces the rich, and declares

emphatically that God's sympathy is with the poor, toward whose needs the rich grow calloused and indifferent. Luke underlines these teachings, not to stir up class division, but to warn that possessions can do deadly damage to man's spiritual life, and to insist that the Church must have a tender concern for the needy and suffering.

3. Equally clear in Jesus' teaching is his friendly interest in the outcasts of society. He cared for the "tax collectors and sinners" (Luke 15: 1). The tax collectors, whose work tied them to the foreign rule of Rome, were despised because they were agents of this pagan power. "Sinners" included people who did not keep the ceremonial rules of Judaism, as well as wrongdoers of every kind. The religious leaders looked down on all such people.

The amazing thing is that while Jesus did not lower his moral standards to those of such outcasts, he was their friend, and they knew it. He gave them hope for a new life and self-respect. In one parable he told how a despised Samaritan gave a wounded traveler the help that the respectable priest and Levite refused (Luke 10: 25-37). In another the prodigal son, returning home penniless and ashamed, received a joyous welcome from his father (Luke 15: 11-32). In such teaching Jesus shows that he sees great possibilities in supposedly hopeless people, and he declares that there is a welcome with God for every man, no matter how bad his past, if he returns to God with sincere regret for his sin and an honest desire to do his Father's will. To make this message plain is one of Luke's aims.

4. The note of Christian joy rings through this Gospel. The angels' song of praise to God in Luke 2: 14 sets the tone of the story. The people who in Jesus have found a new friend and a new life henceforth live in gladness. Not only do men rejoice; heaven and God himself share in the joy over one sinner that repents and finds a new life (Luke 15: 7, 10, 24, 32). What God does for men in Christ is remarkable and thrilling for those who believe; no wonder the story ends with the disciples "in

the temple blessing God" (Luke 24: 53). This is the Gospel of joy; its story brought joy to the writer and will bring joy to every believer.

5. This is the Gospel that stresses prayer. Luke tells more of the prayers of Jesus than the other Gospels do. Jesus is praying at his baptism (Luke 3: 21). After healing the leper he withdraws into the desert and prays (Luke 5: 16). He prays all night before he selects the Twelve and instructs them (Luke 6: 12). His prayer life leads his followers to ask him to teach them to pray (Luke 11: 1). He prays for Peter and for those who crucified him as well as for himself (Luke 22: 32; 23: 34, 46). Prayer was natural and vitally important to Jesus, and the way Luke stresses this fact shows that he too found in prayer an essential of the gospel message and a necessity of the Christian life.

6. The work of the Holy Spirit stands out in Luke more than in any other Gospel. This prepares for the story of The Acts, in which the guidance and power of the Holy Spirit are so prominent. "Full of the Holy Spirit" from the baptism, "led by the Spirit" in the wilderness, taking up his ministry "in the power of the Spirit," Jesus "rejoiced in the Holy Spirit" as he carried on his work (Luke 4: 1, 14; 10: 21). Jesus is thus uniquely bound with the Father and given power for his work.

At the end Jesus instructs his followers that they are to carry on his work in the power of the same Spirit. John the Baptist had promised that the Christ would give the Spirit, and the risen Christ points forward to the realization of that promise, which came at Pentecost (Luke 3: 16; 24: 49). Luke writes after seeing for years that the Church had received the fulfillment of this promise. He bears witness that the work of Jesus and of his followers has been done under the guidance and by the power of the Spirit of God.

The gospel message does not build on the work of man. It is rather the work of God himself. Luke's more frequent references to the Holy Spirit bring out that fact. They help the reader of his Gospel to remember that writer and reader alike depend upon the work and power of God, first through Christ, and then in the Church through the Spirit.

Reading Hints: In reading the first two chapters, give special attention to the hymns: the Magnificat (Luke 1: 46-55), the Benedictus (Luke 1: 68-79), the Gloria in Excelsis (Luke 2: 14), the Nunc Dimittis (Luke 2: 29-32). They express joy, recall how in Christ God fulfilled his promises to Israel, and show the world outreach of the gospel (Luke 2: 14, 32).

Noteworthy Passages and Parables: Jesus in the Temple (Luke 2: 41-52); The Sermon on the Plain (Luke 6: 20-49); The Good Samaritan (Luke 10: 25-37); The Lost Sheep, The Lost Coin, and The Lost Sons (Luke, ch. 15); The Rich Man and Lazarus (Luke 16: 19-31); The Persistent Widow (Luke 18: 1-8); The Pharisee and the Tax Collector (Luke 18: 9-14); The Walk to Emmaus (Luke 24: 13-35).

Nothing takes the place of reading the entire Gospel. The purpose of this book and of these reading hints is to help you to get the most out of reading the New Testament itself.

CHAPTER 6

The Gospel of John

AT THE HIGH POINT of a great drama the lesser actors are usually off the stage. Only the central actors remain in view. This is because the writer of the play does not want the attention of the audience to wander. It must focus on the leading actors and the crucial problem that the play presents.

In much the same way the writer of the Gospel of John concentrates on his central theme. He omits many important things that the other three Gospels contain. Many incidents of Jesus' life and much of Jesus' teaching he does not take time to report. Instead, he centers attention from the start on the heart of the Christian message. He deliberately selects the events and teaching best fitted to make this message clear.

We cannot doubt that this happened. The writer himself says so. In his conclusion to the Gospel story, he states his purpose: "Now Jesus did many other signs in the presence of the disciples, which are not written in this book; but these are written that you may believe that Jesus is the Christ, the Son of God, and that believing you may have life in his name" (John 20: 30, 31). He chooses those events which will best achieve his purpose, which is to tell who Jesus is, what man therefore should do, and what the result of man's response will be.

Who Jesus Is

The writer's basic purpose is to state convincingly who Jesus is. As he preached and taught at the end of the first century, he met people with ideas about Jesus so false that they made Christian faith impossible. For example, the Jews, for the most part, had refused to believe in Jesus. Not all of them had. The first disciples were Jews; the writer of this Gospel is himself a Jew. But the Jewish leaders and most of the Jewish people had rejected Jesus and denied him their faith and obedience. "His own people received him not." (John 1: 11.) Yet he was their Christ and King (John 1: 41, 49).

In addition, there were some, not only in Palestine, but also in other places such as Ephesus (Acts 18: 25; 19: 3), who held that John the Baptist was greater than Jesus. John appeared before Jesus did; he baptized Jesus; so some thought he was the superior one of the two. Yet John himself saw in Jesus one "who ranks before me" (John 1: 30).

Still another view had appeared by the end of the first century. There were people who paid great respect to Jesus, but in a wrong way. They were rather ashamed of Jesus the humble and suffering man, and so they denied he was really a man. He was divine, they said, and only seemed to be human. He had not "become flesh" (cf. John 1: 14); he had not become "wearied" (John 4: 6); he did not really suffer and die on the cross. They said he only seemed to do so. Yet he did become flesh, live a human life, and die a painful death.

Besides these hostile and unworthy attitudes toward Jesus the writer faced the ignorance of many who knew little or nothing at all about Jesus. Men needed to learn the facts and then think clearly about him. They needed to know who he is, so they could take the right attitude toward him.

The faith of the writer himself is clear from the start. Jesus did live in the actual conditions of men, but he was far more than a man. He was a teacher and a prophet, as was John the Baptist, but such titles do not fully explain who he is. He is unique; he is linked with God in life and nature; he is divine.

To leave no doubt concerning this divine nature and supreme importance of Jesus, the writer begins to heap up the high titles of Jesus in the very first chapter. He does not wait, as does Mark, to show how men gradually came to understand who Jesus is; he at once tells the full answer, and continues to emphasize it throughout the Gospel. In this first chapter Jesus is called the "Word" of God, that is, the clear, full expression in human life of the nature and purpose of God (John 1: 1, 14). He is rightly called God (John 1: 1), for he is divine. He is "the Lamb of God," who by his sacrificial death "takes away the sin of the world" (John 1: 29, 36). He is the "Messiah" or "Christ," the "King of Israel" whom the Jews were expecting (John 1: 41, 49). He is the Son of Man (John 1: 51). He is the Son of God (John 1: 49). These dramatic declarations at the opening of the Gospel are continually echoed in later chapters. The climax of the entire story comes when doubting Thomas reverently says to the risen Christ, "My Lord and my God!" (John 20: 28).

What Man Should Do

When men face the divine Son of God, who came and lived and died and rose for them, the only right response is complete faith. The Gospel of John tells the story of how men believed or refused to believe. Some were deceived by the false attractiveness of sin; they "loved darkness rather than light, because their deeds were evil" (John 3: 19). Others were held back by complacent selfishness, as were the grafters Jesus drove from the Temple Court (John 2: 15). Many were too dull to see in Jesus God's new action, God's new challenge and offer to men.

But others, such as Peter and the blind man (John 6: 68, 69; 9: 35-38), were teachable. They saw in the words that Jesus spoke the truth of God, and in the mighty deeds he did they saw the signs that the power of God was present and at work. So they did what God wanted them to do. They believed. They put their faith in Jesus, and lived as his followers. They found that he had the answer to their need.

What Christ Gives to Those Who Believe

What was their need? They needed true life. And through Christ the gift of God to those who believe is life eternal. This Gospel does not speak often of the Kingdom of God, as the other Gospels do. Instead, it speaks frequently of "life" or "eternal life." What does this expression mean? It does not refer merely to physical existence; it means much more than keeping the body alive. It refers to the right kind of life, the life lived in fellowship with God and Christ. "This is eternal life, that they know thee the only true God, and Jesus Christ whom thou hast sent." (John 17: 3.) This life will continue eternally. It is the kind of life that deserves to endure, and the loyal believer may be sure it will.

But it begins now. This point the writer emphasizes. "He who believes in the Son *has* eternal life" now; he who refuses to believe has already shut himself out from the gifts and fellowship of God (John 3: 36). To put faith in Jesus Christ is for a man *the* decisive act of his life—the decisive act of all eternity. It puts him into right relation with God and Christ, so that even death and the final judgment become events of lesser importance than this giving of the life to God. There will be new experiences and added privileges in the time to come, but the essential privilege of living with God through Christ is given to every man as soon as he makes the crucial decision to put his full faith in Christ now and for all time.

This is the central message of the Gospel of John. Jesus is the Christ, the Son of God. He therefore rightly claims the faith and loyalty of every person. To everyone who puts his faith in Christ, full life, eternal life, is God's immediate and permanent gift.

How the Writer Did His Work

To keep attention fastened on this central message, the author omits much that the other Gospels contain. He tells fewer incidents and reports fewer miracles, in order to take more space to point out the meaning of what happened. He recounts almost none of the parables Jesus told; he includes little of the definite teaching Jesus gave his disciples as to how they should act in daily life. Only about eight per cent of this Gospel has any parallel in the other Gospels.

Almost all of the first seventeen chapters is new material. The remaining chapters, which tell of the arrest, trial, death, and resurrection, contain sections found nowhere else, but the earlier chapters are almost entirely new. They begin with a prologue (John 1: 1-18), which states that the person who "became flesh" in Jesus of Nazareth was none other than the divine Word, the eternal Son of God. The story of the public ministry (John 1: 19 to 12: 50) reports mainly the work of Jesus in Judea and especially Jerusalem. It seems clear from the other Gospels that Jesus spent most of his ministry in and around Galilee, but in the Fourth Gospel the visits to Jerusalem at the time of the Jewish feasts claim most attention. That city was the center of Judaism, and there Jesus made his most direct appeal to the leaders of his people. So what happened at Jerusalem receives special notice.

Perhaps the most striking feature of this Gospel is the number of long talks by Jesus. In the other Gospels his sayings are usually brief and concise. So are many sayings in this Gospel, but frequently an event or a meeting leads to a longer discussion. For example, in John, ch. 6, the feeding of the five thousand leads to a talk on Jesus as the Bread of Life. In all these talks the crucial claim of Jesus is the one subject, the choice between faith and unbelief is presented, and eternal life or ruin is at stake. At times these talks bring out the fact that to those with eyes to see the miracles are "signs" of the divine nature and mission of Christ.

These talks all have the same style as do the narratives and the comments of the writer. He has thought long about the meaning of Jesus' life and works. He has often taught the gospel story and what it means for faith. Now, as he writes, he selects instructive events, blends the story and its interpretation, and so brings out the full meaning of what Jesus said and who he was.

No Bible passage is more cherished in the Church than John, chs. 13 to 17, the farewell talks of Jesus with his disciples on the last night of his earthly life. Here what he means to his disciples comes out most clearly. In him God has come to them; he has given them the truth, and the way to life through faith; he has called them together to live in love; he promises to give them the Holy Spirit as their Counselor in all that they do. The Spirit will teach them more fully (as he did the writer of this Gospel) the meaning of the life and work of Christ. Moved by Jesus' life of love for them, they are to live with love for one another and faithfully serve him. Details as to how they should live are not given. What stands out is the great central loyalty to Christ, the great fellowship of Christian love, the great task of leading others to believe in the Son of God. His death will not break the fellowship or defeat his cause; the risen Christ will return to them and give them the Spirit, and they will ever be with him and the Father.

Additions to the Gospel

The writing of the Gospel of John was one of the great events of history. Curiously enough, the original Gospel was enlarged at an early time. Its outline reaches a natural end in the resurrection story in John, ch. 20; the climax comes in the confession of Thomas, "My Lord and my God!" (John 20: 28); a clear and splendid conclusion stands at the end of this chapter (John 20: 30, 31). Chapter 21, then, is a kind of appendix added to the original Gospel. No manuscript of the Gospel lacks this chapter, so it evidently was written and added very early, and the Gospel never circulated without it.

This chapter was added by friends of the witness whose testimony the Gospel contains. This is clear from John 21: 24:

"We know that his testimony is true." In this verse "we" means the friends of the writer; they added the chapter, it appears, shortly after the writer died. Some Christians thought that Jesus had promised this disciple that he would not die (John 21: 23), and one purpose in adding the chapter was to correct a misunderstanding of what Jesus had said.

Quite different is the much later addition of John 7: 53 to 8: 11. This story of a woman taken in sin was no part of the original Gospel of John. But the Church, realizing its value, did not want to lose it; so it was inserted in most late manuscripts of the Gospel of John, although a few manuscripts put it in Luke instead.

The original Gospel of John was written near the close of the first century, and was probably the last of the four Gospels to be prepared. The writer very likely knew the other Gospels, but he also had his own sources of knowledge. In addition, he was an able Christian of independent mind, and felt no need of following literally any written document, however valuable. His Gospel builds mainly upon his own knowledge of the career of Christ. It interprets the meaning of that career for faith; Jesus is the Christ, the Son of God, the giver of eternal life to all who believe.

Who Wrote the Gospel?

That the author was a Jewish Christian is commonly accepted, and rightly so. But he was by no means a narrow partisan of one people. He knew that in God's providence "salvation is from the Jews" (John 4: 22). Yet he also testified that "the hour is coming, and now is, when the true worshipers will worship the Father in spirit and truth"; they need not come to "this mountain" in Samaria or worship "in Jerusalem" (John 4: 21, 23). "God so loved the world that he gave his only Son, that whoever believes in him should not perish but have eternal life" (John 3: 16); "whoever"—whether Jew or Gentile, whether in Palestine or any other land. Although grateful, as Jesus was, for his Jewish heritage, the author saw that all men have a like need and that Christ can meet that need for every man, and so he was able to cross barriers of land and race and speak the universal gospel to the entire world.

This Jewish Christian, ancient tradition says, was John, the son of Zebedee, one of the twelve apostles. It is said that he lived in Ephesus during the last third of the first century, and there, in his old age, wrote not only this Gospel but also the three Epistles of John and the book of The Revelation.

The Gospel itself does not name its author. The appendix, in John 21: 24, identifies him as "the beloved disciple," who is first mentioned in John 13: 23, as present with Jesus at the Last Supper; he appears again in John 19: 26; 20: 2; 21: 7, 20. But he obviously had been a follower of Jesus for some time before the last evening.

Who was this "beloved disciple"? He could have been, as tradition says, John the son of Zebedee. But why, then, if the Galilean fisherman wrote it, does this Gospel center in Jerusalem and not in Galilee, where John lived and worked so much with Jesus? The Galilean ministry and the city where it centered, Capernaum, are hardly mentioned. Could a Judean disciple from Jerusalem or Bethany have written this book?

We know that the tradition was not unchallenged. The first clear statement that John wrote the Gospel comes from the end of the second century. But at that same time other Christians denied that he did. Moreover, while the tradition says that John wrote five books, the book of Revelation differs so much from the Gospel in language, style, and way of thinking that it is most unlikely that both books come from the same author. So the tradition can hardly be entirely right. The three Epistles of John have the same writer as the Gospel, but none of them names its author (the headings were added later). In the two shorter Epistles the writer calls himself "the Elder," a title that marks him as a prominent older Christian leader.

Is there a trustworthy clue here? In the fourth century, Eusebius, quoting the second century Papias, says there was both an apostle John and an Elder John. Shall we conclude from II and III John that the Elder John rather than the apostle John wrote our Gospel?

We cannot answer with certainty. The apostle John may have been the writer, or a follower of his may have written down his gospel story. The Elder John may have written the Gospel, and then in later tradition have been confused with the apostle John. Whether he was John, or a follower of John, or the Elder John, or someone else, the author probably lived in or near Jerusalem before meeting Jesus, and later moved to Ephesus before writing the Gospel.

A True Witness to Christ

Even if we cannot be certain who wrote the Gospel, we know what kind of man he was and what he did. He was an eyewitness of much of Jesus' ministry, or at least he wrote down the clear testimony of such an eyewitness. Back of this book is good information and deep understanding based on close friendship. The writer knew Palestine, its places, its people, its Jewish faith and customs. Though he wrote in a foreign land and in Greek, the atmosphere of the native land of Jesus lingers in his lines.

He was not merely an eyewitness; he was also an interpreter. He knew facts about Jesus' ministry, but he was far more than a reporter. It was his concern to make clear what the facts meant. God gave his Son in order to give life to men. Because Jesus is the Christ, the Son of God, it is possible for men to have life through sincere and active faith in him. The gospel story is thus the offer of salvation; it is the one solid ground of hope. This writer so tells the story that the picture of what Christ did and who Christ is stands clearly before the reader.

In giving this witness the author is simply stating with brilliant skill the common New Testament faith. No one can say that he introduces peculiar notions of his own. No one can claim that he changes the gospel. He states it so that it will be persuasive in the Gentile world where he now is working. But it is the same message that the other Gospels reflect and the rest of the New Testament solidly supports what this Gospel says.

Thus the Gospel of John speaks for the Christian Church of that day and of every generation. It is no wonder that Christians have usually given this book the highest rank. It alone could not be our New Testament; teaching, example, warning, encouragement, promise, and hope come to us from other books in ways we could not do without. But the heart of the Gospel is here: "For God so loved the world that he gave his only Son, that whoever believes in him should not perish but have eternal life" (John 3: 16). And the climax of this Gospel is the true response of faith to Jesus: "My Lord and my God!" (John 20: 28).

Reading Hints: Make a list of all the titles given to Jesus in John, ch. 1. How many other titles are given to him in the rest of the book?

Stories to Remember: Jesus and Nicodemus (John 3: 1-21); Jesus and the Samaritan Woman (John 4: 1-42); The Healing of the Man Born Blind (John, ch. 9); The Raising of Lazarus (John 11: 1-53).

Jesus as the Bread of Life; the Light of the World; the Door; the Good Shepherd; the Resurrection and the Life; the Way, the Truth, and the Life; the True Vine (John 6: 35; 8: 12; 10: 7, 11; 11: 25; 14: 6; 15: 1).

Verses to Know: John 1: 14; 3: 16, 36; 4: 23, 24; 7: 17; 8: 31, 32 (not v. 32 alone!); 13: 34, 35; 20: 30, 31.

Read and reread Jesus' final talk with his disciples and his prayer for them (John, chs. 13 to 17). Note the promise of the sending of the Holy Spirit (John 14: 16, 17, 26; 15: 26; 16: 7, 13).

CHAPTER 7

The Book of The Acts

THE APOSTOLIC CHURCH gave us four Gospels but only one book of The Acts. It is our only connected story of the apostolic age. In later centuries, to be sure, men who had more imagination than information wrote books that they called "Acts." That is, each such writer pretended to tell the story of some favorite apostle. For example, a book appeared that claimed to report "The Acts of Paul." But none of these later writings can be trusted; they contain more fiction than fact. Still later, Christian leaders began to write the history of the Ancient Church, starting with the apostolic age. Their work is valuable, but for knowledge about the apostolic age they had to depend on our book of The Acts.

This book stands alone as the one trustworthy story on which all our later Christian study must build. Without it we could not tell a clear story of the first years of the Church. It tells us the main events that happened; it gives us the message of the first Christian preachers; it provides the setting for the letters of Paul; it lets us see how the Early Church began and grew.

THE ACTS OF THE HOLY SPIRIT

But this is not a story to show what great things brilliant men can do. It was not written to praise human ability and skill. In fact, the usual name of the book, The Acts of the Apostles, is misleading in two respects. First of all, it suggests that this is the story of what all twelve apostles did. The book does speak of the eleven apostles (besides Judas the traitor); it tells also how the twelfth man, Matthias, was chosen to take the place of Judas (Acts 1: 26). Yet most of the Twelve are mentioned only once, in the list of their names (Acts 1: 13), and there are few references to the Twelve as a group. Peter is the only one of these men who plays a notable role in the narrative. The other outstanding leaders in The Acts are not members of the Twelve at all.

But "The Acts of the Apostles" is a misleading title chiefly because it may seem to give all the credit to the human leaders of the Church. In The Acts the story directs attention to the way the Spirit of God guides the disciples in all that they do. The risen Christ, before he leaves his followers at the ascension, promises to send them the Holy Spirit to guide and uphold them. At Pentecost he sends the Spirit to the waiting, worshiping Church, and from that time the Spirit leads them. At every decisive step the story refers to his guidance. This book is really "The Acts of the Holy Spirit," who carries out God's work through human agents.

The Meaning of Pentecost

Because the Spirit is the leading actor of the book, the story of Pentecost fits well at the start. This account, in Acts, ch. 2, tells a striking story of great excitement when the disciples were filled with the Spirit. As a result, many Christians think that what occurred was only a thrilling emotional experience, which gave great joy to the disciples. It was that, of course, and the note of joy sounds frequently in The Acts (Acts 16: 34). Not even persecution dampened the glad and courageous spirit of Christ's followers (Acts 5: 41). But the real point of the story is that God sent his Spirit into the Church, and from that time it spoke and acted with courage and power.

The disciples had been waiting. They had not taken up the active work of Christ. Then the Spirit came; they became vigorously active; their leaders could not be silenced or intimidated. The power to speak, to act, to heal, to persevere—this the Spirit gave them. They did not face the world or do their work in their own strength. The Spirit of God was with them to give joy and power and direction. Pentecost changed the group of waiting disciples into the active Church of Christ.

Christian Worship

What, then, was the life of the Church like in those early days? The story by Luke shows that three essentials of a live and working Church were present.

Of first importance was continual, grateful worship. It was out of true faith and willing worship that the work of the disciples grew. We recall that at the start it was while waiting and worshiping that they received the Spirit. As Peter and John went to the Temple to share in Jewish worship of God they found the first opportunity to heal (Acts 3: 1). When these same two leaders, threatened by the Jewish rulers, returned to the disciples, the Church's response to threats and danger was to pray and commit their lives to God (Acts 4: 23-31). It was while the Church was praying at the home of Mary the mother of Mark that Peter was released from prison (Acts 12: 12). The leaders of the Antioch church were praying when the call came to send out Barnabas and Saul for missionary work (Acts 13: 2). Throughout the history of the Apostolic Church, the grateful worship of God was basic; all that the disciples were able to do grew out of their glad and reverent worship of the God and Father of the Lord Jesus Christ.

We should notice that this was common worship regularly shared. At times individuals prayed alone; thus Peter, praying on the housetop at Joppa (Acts 10: 9), was led to go to Caesarea and preach to Gentiles in the household of Cornelius. But the regular practice was to pray and to praise God together. Private prayer was never a substitute for this faithful meeting with other Christians for united worship of God.

Christian Fellowship

As important as worship was the close friendship between the disciples. Its first expression, in frequent common worship, is the more remarkable because danger of persecution might have made Christians hesitate to let others see their Christian loyalty. But they did not hold back or hide. They met together regularly to worship. These meetings included a common meal whenever possible; "the breaking of bread" (Acts 2: 42) recalled the death of Christ and what his coming and death meant for their salvation.

Such fellowship gave to believers the companionship they needed. Many outsiders were suspicious and even hostile, and it was a comfort and a source of strength for a disciple to have comrades who stood steadfast with him. To be sure, these fellow Christians had their weaknesses. Is this surprising? Remember what kind of people we are. Recall that it is not perfect men but sinful people whom the gospel invites to give up wrong ways and enter the Church to rebuild life in loyalty to Christ. The first Christians were not perfect. But the disciples knew where help was to be found. It was with God and in the company of Christ's people. Those outside the Church were no source of strength for faith or life. They were indifferent or hostile to Christ the Lord. The one truly good and helpful fellowship was that between the followers of the Master.

This was a fellowship in learning. Disciples needed to learn more about Christ's life and work, more of what those facts teach about faith and living. So they "devoted themselves to the apostles' teaching and fellowship" (Acts 2: 42). Teachers were active as time went on; at Antioch, for example, there were "prophets and teachers" (Acts 13: 1), of whom Barnabas and Saul were two. To be a Christian was to grow in knowledge of Christ and of the light the gospel throws on daily life. This made the fellowship of learning a necessity.

The fellowship led also to a sharing of food with disciples in need. This help to the hungry sometimes has been called "Christian communism," but this term is very misleading. Today the word "Communism" suggests denial that God exists. It implies that the State has total control over all of life, and in particular that the State has full charge of producing and distributing material goods. The situation in the Early Church was entirely different. What did happen?

The city of Jerusalem has never been self-supporting. Many of the first Christians were Galileans, with no business ties in Jerusalem to enable them to make a living. Hostility and persecution made their financial lot still harder. Famine later made their need even more acute. Add to these difficulties the fact that the gospel was preached to the poor from the start. Jesus had great sympathy with the needy, and the disciples welcomed them into the Church. Later, as the gospel spread through the Roman Empire, the Christians appealed to all classes, including slaves; we find many poor people and numerous slaves in the Christian group.

These things explain what happened. Most of the disciples in Jerusalem were very poor. Those who were better off were too Christian to let their fellow Christians starve. They gave money and goods, and sometimes even sold their property (Acts 4: 34-37), to help the poor in their group. They were not planning with a long view, it is true, and they thought the end of this age was not far off. But the main point is clear: the faith produced a fellowship so vital that it willingly helped those who were in need.

Hospitality was another expression of Christian fellowship. As the Church spread, its leaders—Paul, for example—journeyed from place to place. Then, too, Christians traveled on business, or moved from one place to another, as Priscilla and Aquila did when forced to move from Rome to Corinth and when they moved later to Ephesus (Acts 18: 2, 18, 19). The inns were often immoral places, and so local Christians gave hospitality in their homes to Christian visitors. It was a practice that helped to bind the local church together with the one great brotherhood of Christ; it helped each group to realize that it was part of the great world Church.

Christian Witness

The Apostolic Church always had as its aim the giving of faithful witness to the gospel. The Church is not established to think selfishly of its own desires. Its task, under the guidance of the Holy Spirit, is to witness to Christ and to grow in numbers as well as in faith. It may suffer setbacks; it may be persecuted and seem for a time to fail. But it is to tell other men the gospel of Christ, in the faith that the Lord, in his wisdom and by his Spirit, will keep adding to the Church those who receive the Christian testimony (Acts 2: 47).

The apostles first of all had this task (Acts 1: 1-8). They were to tell what God had done for men in Christ. To do this they must tell the story from the appearance of John the Baptist to the resurrection of Christ; particularly important was the witness to the resurrection (Acts 1: 22). This witness the apostles gave with power (Acts 4: 33); they even refused to clutter their lives with other work, however important (Acts 6: 1-4).

Yet many others besides the Twelve gave the same witness. Even among the Seven, chosen to care for needy people, we find first Stephen and then Philip active in preaching (Acts 6: 9, 10; 8: 5). Others, whose names we do not know, carried the gospel to an ever-widening field; for example, those driven from Jerusalem by persecution preached in Phoenicia, Cyprus, and Antioch (Acts 11: 19, 20).

Outline of The Acts

If we prepare an outline of the book of The Acts, we see how this witness was given. There is more than one way to make such an outline, and each one will teach us something important.

1. In the first twelve chapters Peter is the dominant figure and Palestine the main place of interest. Paul takes the center of the stage in the last sixteen chapters, and the missionary work spreading out from Antioch in Syria is the focus of attention.

2. We can sketch the growth of the Church more closely by following the work of six main leaders. Peter comes first. He was the vigorous spokesman not only for the Twelve but for the entire group at Jerusalem. Standing firm against threats, beatings, and imprisonment, he dominates the first five chapters and is prominent in chapters nine through twelve. He is the only one of the Twelve who plays a vital personal role in the account of The Acts. The others were good and useful leaders, but we hear only of Peter's individual action.

To minister to the Greek-speaking Jews and to help the poor, the Church, at the suggestion of the Twelve, chose the Seven (Acts, ch. 6). Two of them, Stephen and Philip, did outstanding work. Stephen was the most active and outspoken (Acts 6: 8 to 8: 1). He had caught from Jesus the truth that the Temple, respected as it had deserved to be, was not necessary to true worship; he prepared the way for the wider mission of the Church, although he himself did not undertake it, but soon died for his faith. Philip, by preaching in Samaria and along the coastal region of Palestine (Acts 8: 5-40), began an expanding work that was to take the Church far beyond the limits of a purely Jewish group.

A fourth key leader was Barnabas. Though never a powerful speaker, he was a man of deep faith and was ready at personal cost to help the poor (Acts 4: 36, 37). He sensed the genuineness of Paul's conversion and vouched for him (Acts 9: 27). The Jerusalem church trusted him to go to Antioch and see whether the conversion of the Gentiles there was genuine, and the Antioch church accepted him as a leader (Acts 11: 22-26). He, not Paul, is named as leader of the first missionary journey from Antioch (Acts 13: 2). Paul forged ahead in the course of this journey, but Barnabas took the lead when they went back to Jerusalem to defend the admission of Gentiles into the churches (Acts 15: 12, 25). Soon after, he drops out of our sight, but he had been the wise and most trusted pioneer leader who first guided the Church as it expanded from its Jewish Palestinian home into the wider Roman world.

Among Jewish Christians who continued to feel strong loyalty to the Jewish law and tradition the outstanding leader was James the brother of the Lord. Some have thought him one of the Twelve; this does not seem correct. But he was in the Church from its earliest days. Though not a follower of Jesus during his earthly ministry (John 7: 5), he was one of those who saw the risen Christ (I Cor. 15: 7), and was a member of the Jerusalem church from the beginning (Acts 1: 13). At first the Twelve, with Peter prominent, headed the Church, but the special reference to James in Acts 12: 17 shows that by then he had become recognized as a leader, and when the conference as to the place of Gentiles in the Church was held, he presided and stated the decision that was passed (Acts 15: 13-21). On Paul's last visit to Jerusalem, James appears as the leader there (Acts 21: 18). He was known as James the Just, an honest and steadfast Christian, who died as a martyr about A.D. 62.

But he suffered from limited spiritual vision. He could see a place for Gentiles in the Church, but he did not want Jewish Christians to associate freely with them (Gal. 2: 11). He had no part in the widening mission to all peoples; he himself remained bound to conservative Jewish practices. He was a great man, a respected leader, but he never really saw how free and universal the gospel is.

The man with the clear understanding, burning devotion, unswerving persistence, and powerful witness to make the Christian movement a world force was the apostle Paul. Even Peter, though led to receive into the Church the household of the Gentile Cornelius, was still hesitant, and he worked, as Paul states, chiefly among the Jews (Gal. 2: 9, 12). Paul, a

Jew who loved his people and was heartbroken that so many of them would not believe in Christ, was the one who pushed forward to present the gospel to the entire Mediterranean world. His work, with its world vision, is the center of interest in the latter half of The Acts. Of the six great leaders, he saw the task most clearly.

3. Still another way to outline The Acts is to follow the geographical expansion. First comes the story of the Church at Jerusalem (Acts 1: 1 to 6: 7). Then follows the spread throughout Palestine (Acts 6: 8 to 9: 31). The third part reports the extension to Antioch in Syria (Acts 9: 32 to 12: 24). In the fourth division the Church spreads to Asia Minor (Acts 12: 25 to 16: 5). Part five tells of its extension to Macedonia and Greece in Europe (Acts 16: 6 to 19: 20). The last part tells how Paul the prisoner reaches Rome with the gospel (Acts 19: 21 to 28: 31).

As a general picture, this outline serves well. But the divisions are not rigid, and there are some stages that it does not report. For example, there was a church in Damascus before Paul went there (Acts 9: 2, 19), yet The Acts does not tell who carried the gospel there. In Rome too, and other Italian cities, there were churches before Paul reached that region (Acts 28: 13-15), but The Acts gives no record of how the gospel came to Italy.

With Paul's preaching at Rome the book of The Acts closes. His missionary preaching in the capital city of the Empire is a symbol of the fact that the gospel is going into all parts of the world. Its world outreach has become clear. It is going "to the end of the earth" (Acts 1: 8).

How Luke Wrote The Acts

In studying the Gospels we saw that Luke-Acts was originally one work. It described the beginnings of Christianity, from the birth of John the Baptist and Jesus to the arrival of Paul at Rome. Its author was Luke the beloved physician. As traveling companion of Paul and a visitor in Palestine for at least two years, he had been well situated to learn about the career of Christ and the earliest days of the Church.

Did Luke find written records to help him in the writing of The Acts? Perhaps he did, and the way he used such sources in writing his Gospel shows that he would have been ready to use good sources if available. The "we" passages in The Acts, in which the writer appears to include himself among those present with Paul (Acts 16: 10-17; 20: 5-15; 21: 1-18; and 27: 1 to 28: 16), may come from a diary Luke himself had kept of his travels with the apostle. One thing is clear. The narrative is less complete in the earlier chapters, which cover ground that Luke knew only indirectly. In the later chapters, which tell of Paul, Luke can write with more detailed knowledge, and gives a more connected story.

When did Luke write the book of The Acts? Some have thought that he wrote at the end of the two years Paul spent in prison at Rome (Acts 28: 30), before it was known how Paul's trial there would come out. The date of The Acts would then be about A.D. 63. But Luke, in writing his Gospel, used the Gospel of Mark as a source, so we must date both Luke and The Acts later than Mark. Ancient tradition tells us that Mark wrote after the death of Peter (A.D. 64 or 67), so his Gospel can hardly be dated earlier than A.D. 65 to 70. The date of Luke and The Acts must be still later, and we may place the writing of The Acts about A.D. 85.

The Purpose of Luke

Luke's main purpose is clear. He gives the story of the rise and spread of the gospel until it becomes a world faith. He follows it until it is established in Rome and is spreading through the Roman Empire and beyond. In telling this story of what God did through Christ and the Holy Spirit, he aims to give Christians a trustworthy record of the story on which their faith and hope must always rest.

But Luke has other lesser aims. He is careful to point out that the Christians, like Jesus himself, were not guilty of any wrongdoing. Their enemies often charged that they were rebels against Rome and disturbers of the peace. Luke shows that the disciples and especially their leaders were upright and deserved Roman respect and protection. The gospel they brought changed men, to be sure, but it saved them and led them to live better lives, so no one could rightly condemn it.

Luke also emphasizes the fact that Christianity is the true Judaism. Jesus is the Christ of the Jewish hope. The disciples were faithful Jews; they wanted to continue to worship in Temple and synagogue; only the bitter hostility and persecution they suffered from unbelieving Jews drove them to live and worship separately. The Church fulfilled the Jewish Scriptures, and so, because it carried forward God's work with Israel, the Roman Empire should protect the Church as it had been protecting Judaism.

But these were lesser points. The chief aim of Luke was to tell clearly the gospel story and to show that this gospel was not only the true Judaism but also the right faith for all men. He gave his witness to all readers that since in Christ God had acted for their salvation, the fellowship of the one world Church was now open to all who would believe. And he reminded the Church that its task is to carry the gospel of Christ into all the world.

READING HINTS: In reading The Acts, remember that here Luke continues the story he had begun in his Gospel. This too is part of God's redemptive work. Keep in mind Acts 1: 8.

Study the spread of the gospel by noting the six sections of the book and the summary at the end of each (Acts 6: 7; 9: 31; 12: 24; 16: 5; 19: 20; 28: 30, 31).

Special Stories: Pentecost (Acts 2: 1-41); The Story of Stephen (Acts 6: 1 to 8: 3); The Conversion of Paul (Acts 9: 1-22); Peter and Cornelius (Acts 10: 1 to 11: 18); The Conference at Jerusalem (Acts 15: 1-35); The Conversion of the Philippian Jailer (Acts 16: 16-34); The Shipwreck of Paul (Acts, ch. 27).

CHAPTER 8

The Christian Letter Writer

NO ONE could ever ignore Paul. The early Christians at Jerusalem learned that; he persecuted them. Once he became a Christian, the Jews in city after city found that he would not let them alone. He insisted that they face the claim of the gospel of Christ. Wherever he went he made people pay attention to him. He had energy; he was never neutral; he stood with all his strength for what he believed. Men argued with him, denounced him, imprisoned and beat and stoned him, but they found that they could not ignore him.

The book of The Acts helps to make this plain. Paul is one of the two outstanding figures in its story of the Apostolic Church. To his work as preacher and missionary The Acts gives more space than it does to any other apostle. Then, too, almost half the writings of the New Testament come from his pen. He never dreamed that we would still be reading them nineteen hundred years after he wrote them, but this very fact just shows again that Paul is a man who demands attention.

It is especially because of these letters that Paul is still important in the Church. We must study them to understand him well. Now a letter, by its very nature, grows out of a definite situation. To understand it we need to know the writer and the situation in which he wrote it. For this reason we must make a brief survey of Paul's career. This will help us to see why he wrote letters and what he expected them to achieve. They grew out of the Christian work he was doing.

Saul the Jew

Paul had two names, and each reflects one background of his life. His Jewish parents, who lived in southeastern Asia Minor, in the Gentile city of Tarsus (Acts 22: 3), had named him Saul, after the first king of Israel. Loyal to their Jewish faith, they brought Paul up to be equally devoted to it (Phil. 3: 5). As a resident in a Gentile city, he learned Greek, and this prepared him for his later missionary work. But he also learned both the Hebrew in which the Jewish Scriptures had first been written and, in addition, the Aramaic which most people in Palestine spoke. In his youth he went to Jerusalem to study. In fierce, undivided loyalty to his ancestral faith, he became a Pharisee, as his father had been before him (Acts 23: 6). By residence in Tarsus and by travel he knew something of pagan life and religion, but this made him only more determined to be completely true to his Jewish faith. His earnest life made him an outstanding Jew (Gal. 1: 13, 14).

His Roman name, Paul, which he used in his missionary work, recalls that he was a Roman citizen, as his father also had been (Acts 16: 37; 22: 25-28). How his family received this rank we cannot say, but it proved useful to him: he could appeal to it to stop illegal mistreatment by hostile officials (Acts 16: 37-39; 22: 25-28; 25: 11). Yet his pride in this citizenship never made Paul ashamed of his Jewish faith. His one deep loyalty was to the God of Israel and the law of Moses.

The Persecutor

When the young Pharisee Saul first met the Christians, he saw in them a threat to Judaism. He sensed the fact that to give Christ first place would change the Jewish way of life; perhaps he already began to see that it would open the way for Gentiles to share the gospel. So he fought the Christians. He was never one to do things by halves. He began a vigorous attempt to stamp out the new Church (Gal. 1: 13). He was present at the death of Stephen, whose mob murder he approved. Searching out Christians, he dragged them off to prison (Acts 8: 1-3).

Nor did he stop with such action at Jerusalem. He learned that the Christian movement was spreading and had taken root in Damascus, so he decided to go there to fight it. Since Damascus was not a Jewish region, he took with him letters from the high priest to the Damascus rulers, and set out on his journey (Acts 9: 1, 2).

Christian Convert and Preacher

He set out as a persecutor of the Church, but he arrived as a Christian. On the way the risen Christ met him, and Saul the persecutor yielded his life to the Jesus he had so bitterly denounced (Acts 9: 1-19). He learned that these Christians were not deluded fools but "the church of God" (I Cor. 15: 9). Always a man to act vigorously and promptly, he at once joined the very group he had come to persecute.

This was not all he did. He went off into Arabia, south of Damascus, for a short time (Gal. 1: 17). Perhaps while there he began to preach. Certainly as soon as he returned to Damascus he boldly preached to his Jewish hearers that Jesus is the Christ and that all Jews should believe in him (Acts 9: 20-22). Those who heard him treated him as he had intended to treat the Damascus Christians. They plotted to get rid of him. But he learned of this, and, with the help of his fellow Christians, who lowered him from a window in the city wall, he escaped (Acts 9: 23-25; II Cor. 11: 32, 33).

Yet he did not seek a safe and quiet place. Instead, he went to Jerusalem. There he had persecuted the disciples; he now wanted to join them, meet Peter (Gal. 1: 18, 19), and tell his fellow Jews that the Christian faith is true. This was dangerous, but he considered it his Christian duty. It surprised the disciples when he returned, and until Barnabas assured them that Paul's conversion was genuine, they feared that it was another trick of their former persecutor (Acts 9: 26-30).

Within two weeks the hostility of the Jews who heard him preach became so dangerous that his new Christian friends took him to Caesarea and sent him to Tarsus.

This did not stop his work. He could not stay silent or inactive. We hear later of churches in Cilicia (Acts 15: 41). Evidently Paul preached in Tarsus and other nearby places with success. In the meantime, Barnabas had not forgotten him. He no doubt heard of Paul's preaching (Gal. 1: 23), and when the new church at Antioch in Syria needed help he went to Tarsus and convinced Paul that his task was at Antioch. There Paul went and became a leader as a prophet and teacher (Acts 13: 1).

A Missionary Sent from Antioch

After a short visit to Jerusalem to take relief when famine threatened the Christians there (Acts 11: 27-30), the Spirit of God led Paul into a wider missionary work. Not from the twelve apostles, but from the "prophets and teachers" at Antioch, came this decision that was to change the world. In their worship they were led to set apart Barnabas, their older, trusted leader, and Saul, their vigorous younger worker, for preaching in other places. And so, like Abraham, who long before "went out, not knowing where he was to go" (Heb. 11: 8), Barnabas and Saul, with John Mark as helper, set out.

They went first to a region Barnabas knew, that is, to Cyprus, his birthplace (Acts 4: 36). Their first preaching was to Jews there. Later, after they crossed to Asia Minor and went inland to Antioch of Pisidia, the opposition of the Jews led them to "turn to the Gentiles" (Acts 13: 46). They never stopped preaching to the Jews, wherever the Jews would listen. But repeatedly the missionaries were driven from the synagogues, and they spoke to men of all races on the streets, in private homes, or in rented halls.

Upon leaving Cyprus for Asia Minor, Paul stepped into the place of leadership, and Mark, perhaps because of resentment at Paul, went home. Opposition and even persecution met the apostles in more than one city, but they preached in Antioch, Iconium, Lystra, and Derbe in central Asia Minor before they went back to the southern coast. Then they returned to Antioch in Syria to report their success in winning converts to Christ (Acts, chs. 13; 14).

One Church for All

At Antioch, Jews and Gentiles were united in one church. On their missionary journey, Paul and Barnabas found Gentiles even more ready than Jews to accept the gospel. It was becoming clear that the gospel had a message for all men. But for Jews this raised a serious problem—the problem of the Jewish law. The Jews felt that the law, as set forth in the first five books of their Scripture, and as interpreted in the unwritten traditions that the scribes handed on, was absolutely basic in their faith. Their hope of remaining in right relationship to God rested on faithful obedience to the rules and regulations that had been given to them.

The Jewish law contained ceremonies and rites that separated them from the Gentile world. In times past this law had kept the Jews from sharing in the idol worship and immorality of the pagan world. Now that faith in Christ had come to unite men in one brotherhood under the one God, what was to become of the law?

The test case was circumcision. Jews were willing to receive Gentiles into the Church, if they would become circumcised and keep the prominent ceremonial requirements of the law. For all practical purposes they were requiring converts to become Jews in order that they might become Christians. This Paul had not required of Gentiles. To him, the gospel meant that no external rite or practice is essential for salvation. Men are all sinners; they cannot save themselves; their hope comes only from the free gift of God. If their salvation depended on keeping the law of Moses, as was argued by those who demanded circumcision of the Gentiles, then no one could be saved. All men sin, and so, under a law that gives rewards only to those who obey it, all will be condemned. Since, then, no man can keep this law, and both Jews and Gentiles must trust God for forgiveness and the gifts needed to find new life, the demand for circumcision and keeping the law is not only futile but dangerous. It obscures the grace of God; it leads a man to try to keep a law which, because he is a sinner, he can never really keep; it suggests that he should trust in what he does, when his only possible hope and trust is in God. So what Paul asked of Gentiles was only sincere faith in Christ, and a life of Christian love and obedience which the Spirit gives power to live.

When this issue was sharply raised at Antioch in Syria, the leaders took it to Jerusalem for conference with the leaders there (Gal. 2: 1-10; Acts 15: 1-29). The decision was that Gentile Christians do not have to accept circumcision and keep the ceremonial rules to be saved. A temporary ruling warned against lax sex standards, and especially asked the Gentile Christians to observe certain food laws and customs so as not to offend their Jewish fellow Christians (Acts 15: 20, 29). This was like not serving meat on Friday when some present are Roman Catholics. But in essentials Paul's position was approved; Gentiles need not keep the Jewish law.

Paul's Wider Mission Work

This decision opened the way to further missionary work. After revisiting the churches in central Asia Minor, Paul went northwest to Troas, crossed to Europe, and worked successively in Philippi, Thessalonica, Berea, Athens, and Corinth (Acts 15: 36 to 18: 22). In this latter city he wrote First and Second Thessalonians; and it may have been at Corinth that he wrote his letter to the Galatians. A brief visit to Ephesus and then to Jerusalem, followed by a trip back to Syrian Antioch, concluded this first half of his wider work.

In all that Paul had done he had shown an eye for strategy.

He went to the great centers, the key cities. There he planted churches; from them the gospel was carried out into the surrounding regions. Quite likely Paul sent out helpers into such regions to establish churches in smaller cities.

When he again left Antioch, he first traveled through Asia Minor to revisit the churches there, and then stopped in Ephesus, where he made the longest stay of his wider mission work (Acts 18: 23 to 19: 41). There he wrote First Corinthians; and it was either at Ephesus or at Corinth two years earlier that he wrote to the Galatians. At the end of three busy years, during which he made a quick trip to Corinth and perhaps other side journeys, he went north through Asia Minor, revisited Macedonia, where he wrote Second Corinthians, and went on to Greece, where he wrote Romans. After three months he returned through Macedonia, sailed down the western coast of Asia Minor, and went on to Jerusalem for the Feast of Pentecost (Acts 20: 1 to 21: 16). He took with him a large collection from his Gentile churches to the needy Jewish Christians in Jerusalem (I Cor. 16: 1-4; II Cor., chs. 8; 9; Rom. 15: 25-27; Acts 24: 17). By this expression of Christian sympathy and sharing he hoped to bind together the two parts of the one Christian Church. After that he hoped to preach in Spain.

The old Jewish hostility against Paul shattered his plans. While he was in the Temple, fanatics raised a riot against him and tried to take his life. The Roman soldiers who rescued him held him under arrest, and though he was innocent of any crime, he was kept a prisoner at Caesarea for two years (Acts 21: 17 to 24: 27). Even then, to avoid being taken back to Jerusalem, where Jews had made plots to kill him, he had to appeal to the Roman emperor for a fair trial in Rome. On the way there, he suffered shipwreck on the island of Malta (Acts, chs. 25 to 28).

In Rome, Paul spent two years in prison waiting for trial (Acts 28: 30), and probably during that period he wrote Philemon, Colossians, Ephesians, and Philippians. The book of The Acts does not tell the result of his trial. An ancient tradition says that he was released and did further Christian work before being again arrested and put to death at Rome on suspicion of being dangerous to the Empire. Only in this later period can we find a place for the writing of the letters to Timothy and Titus.

Pastor by Letter

In all this travel Paul combined two kinds of work. He was constantly taking the gospel into new regions. He was a missionary, the greatest the Church has known. But he was also a pastor at heart; he never forgot the Christians in the churches he had founded, and in faithful love for them he took every opportunity to revisit them and help them in their Christian life.

But his visits alone were not enough to guide these new and inexperienced churches. These visits were too few and too short, and he could not always make them when the churches most needed him. So he used two other ways to send help. One was to send a trusted assistant to help a perplexed, divided, or persecuted church. The other was to write letters. No Christian ever used the letter more effectively to advance the cause of Christ. It is these letters that we are now to study.

And they are real letters. Paul was not writing general books on Christian teaching. In each letter he was trying to meet the specific needs of a definite group or person. He spoke directly and frankly. What he said grew out of a specific situation.

Letters, of course, were nothing new. In the dry sands of Egypt thousands of ancient letters have been found, usually written upon papyrus. They deal with all sorts of problems and situations, and many were private, informal letters of common folk. But scholars and rulers sometimes wrote more formal letters; they often kept copies of such letters and published them in book form.

Paul's letters are more like the letters of common people than the formal letters of ancient scholars and rulers. He wrote with the same directness, the same lack of concern for literary greatness, that we find in everyday letters. Though he was not careless, as were some ancient letter writers, he had the same vital touch with a living situation, the same frank and personal expression, that marked their letters. His interest was centered in what he had to say much more than in clever ways to say it.

How Paul Used the Letter Pattern

In Paul's day as in ours, there were common patterns used in writing letters. He followed the usual form. But in content his letters are unlike anything ever found in the sands of Egypt. At every stage he gives a Christian turn to what he says.

The ordinary Greek letter opened with the pattern: "A to B, greeting." Paul comes closest to this formula in First and Second Thessalonians, but always he expands it and makes it Christian. Sometimes he tells something of his Christian calling; sometimes he adds remarks in praise of those to whom he writes; always his word of greeting goes beyond mere form to give a Christian prayer for God's gifts to his readers. These Christian additions are longest in Romans, First Corinthians, and Galatians, but every letter has them, and we should compare the openings of them all to see how Paul's faith always finds expression.

The next part of a Greek letter was a section of thanks, personal appreciation, and prayer for the reader or readers. Paul has this in every letter except Galatians. There, shocked by the failure of the Galatians to hold fast to the true gospel, Paul at once plunges into a sharp rebuke (Gal. 1: 6-10). The readers, expecting some word of friendliness or prayer for them, must have been startled by this blunt rebuke so unexpectedly spoken. In other letters, however, Paul follows the usual custom. Even in First Corinthians, where he must include much correction and rebuke, he first thanks God for the gifts and good points of the Corinthians before he proceeds to teach and correct them.

After the thanksgiving the Greek letter came to its main section, and here the writer's purpose guided what he said. In the case of Paul, it is clear that he always deals with the needs of his churches. His purpose is not only to guide them in true faith but also to direct them in right Christian living. Repeatedly he points out what the gospel means in terms of human relations and personal actions. To him these things were essential parts of the Christian life, and especially at the end of the letters he gives valuable teaching on such questions.

The typical Greek letter ended with personal greetings and the word "farewell." Paul usually has such greetings. Since his habit is to dictate his letters, he often takes the pen and adds a personal note in his own handwriting. This was a friendly expression and enabled friends to know his genuine letters (II Thess. 3: 17). His final word of greeting was not the formal "farewell" but a Christian prayer of benediction. It always included the prayer that the free grace of God might continually be given to the readers.

One Gospel for Many Situations

As we now go on to study Paul's letters, trying to follow the order in which they were written, we may be surprised by the variety of problems they contain and by the appearance in each letter of new ideas we have not heard from Paul before. Did he keep changing his ideas? That would be a false conclusion. We must remember that he had been a Christian for at least fifteen years before he wrote the earliest letter we now have. He had been preaching and teaching and thinking for a long time. He was no newcomer to the Church, no novice in Christian work. So his earliest letter was not from an immature beginner. It came from an experienced leader.

The differences between the letters, then, are due mainly to the different situations. In all the letters, Paul writes of the same Christian gospel and with the same Christian purpose. But in each case a new set of problems confronts him. He deals with each new situation as it arises; he does not try to put into each letter all that he believes and knows.

Often this makes it hard for us to understand the letter, and we may wish that he had said more, so that we could see the total picture of what he thought. But we must take each letter as it stands. We must try to understand the situation in which it was written, and see how Paul used the gospel to meet that situation. Then we can put the letters together and get a fairly full picture of Paul's faith and thought.

We then can also see what they mean to us. The Church preserved these letters and put them into the New Testament because it saw that what Paul said in the first century is full of help to later generations. Through these letters God can lead us, as Paul's readers were led, to find the way to Christian faith and life.

READING HINTS: On the life of Paul, read the speeches in Acts 20: 17-38; 22: 1-21; 26: 1-29, and Paul's review of his life in Gal., chs. 1 and 2.

To see the pattern used in letters, read Acts 15: 23-29; 23: 26-30.

For a hint of the energy and activity of Paul, read II Cor. 6: 3-10; 11: 23-28.

CHAPTER 9

Two Letters to Thessalonica

TRAVELING on foot, Paul and Silas came to Thessalonica. They had been driven from Philippi. There Paul had restored to sanity a slave girl used in fortunetelling, and her owners had caused him to be beaten, thrown into prison, and put in chains. Though the rulers later apologized, they insisted that Paul and Silas leave the city before more trouble arose. So the two Christian missionaries traveled west until they came to Thessalonica.

Why did they stop there? It was just such a city as Paul often chose for his work. He made it his rule to preach in the great cities, from which the gospel could spread into the smaller places round about. Thessalonica was such a center of population, trade, and travel. To the north lay a fertile valley and important roads for trade. Through the city from east to west ran the famous Egnatian Way, the main Roman road of that area. On the south was the Aegean Sea, and Thessalonica, with its excellent harbor, had a lively sea trade. Here Paul stopped to establish a church.

How Paul Founded the Church

In such a city Paul first looked for the synagogue. Business and trade openings had drawn many Jews to Thessalonica, so he soon found their place of worship. There were gathered not only Jews, but also many Gentiles, especially Gentile women, attracted by the high faith and moral standards that marked the Jewish people. This situation suited Paul perfectly. He knew that Christ came "to the Jew first," so he never neglected to preach to the Jews, but he himself was sent especially to the Gentiles, and those whom he found in the synagogues were best prepared to hear his story. They already knew the Old Testament and the faith of the Jews, and were ready to listen to his story about Jesus Christ.

So, "as was his custom," Paul visited the synagogue, and "for three weeks [sabbaths] he argued with them from the scriptures, explaining and proving that it was necessary for the Christ to suffer and to rise from the dead, and saying, 'This Jesus, whom I proclaim to you, is the Christ'" (Acts 17: 2, 3). He won both Jews and "Greeks," that is, Gentiles. A small but earnest Christian church was formed.

How long did Paul stay in Thessalonica? In The Acts, Luke tells of only three weeks of synagogue preaching, followed by a riot which forced Paul to leave. This sounds as if he stayed no more than a month. But Luke's practice is to tell only two things about the work Paul did in a city: he tells how Paul began, and what led him to move on to the next place. Paul's own statement that the Christians at Thessalonica "turned to God from idols" (I Thess. 1: 9) shows that most of them were Gentiles who had worshiped idols rather than the one God of Israel. The contrast between them and the Jewish Christians in Palestine is more proof that most of their number were Gentiles (I Thess. 2: 14). This means that Paul stayed much longer than The Acts suggests; his preaching in the synagogue was only the first part of his mission work in that city. How long he stayed we do not know; it may have been several months.

Jewish hostility stirred up a riot and forced him to leave. Though the mob could not find Paul and Silas, it seized some Christians, including Jason, Paul's host, and dragged them before the city rulers. The mob cried that Paul and Silas were rebels who wanted to make Jesus king and so overthrow

Roman rule. This charge gave a political twist to the Christian faith in Christ as the Lord of life; it wrongly accused Paul of plotting political revolution. The officials were alarmed; they made Jason give bond that there would be no more disturbance (Acts 17: 5-9). This forced Paul to leave the city. Had he continued preaching, further riots would have occurred and the rulers would have taken stern action.

From Thessalonica, Paul went first to Berea and then to Athens. With deep interest in the young church, and because he knew that opposition and persecution still troubled the Christians in Thessalonica, he sent Timothy back to see how their faith was holding up. Before Timothy returned, Paul had gone on to Corinth. It was there that Timothy brought him the good news that they were standing firm in faith and remembered Paul with love and gratitude (I Thess. 3: 1-8).

The First Letter

These Christians needed friendship; they needed teaching and encouragement. Plainly, they longed to see Paul again. He too wanted to see them, but something prevented his return (I Thess. 2: 17, 18; 3: 6). Probably it was the bond Jason had given; even though Paul would not start another riot, he would be held responsible, and his friends would suffer, if he returned and further trouble occurred.

A letter was now his best substitute for a visit. Sending Timothy had been a help and had shown his love, but now he wanted not only to express in his own words his joy at their steadfastness but also to give them needed teaching. So at Corinth, about A.D. 51, Paul wrote the letter we call First Thessalonians. He courteously included Silvanus (Silas) and Timothy as coauthors, but it is really Paul's letter. He dictated it.

It has two parts. In the first one (I Thess., chs. 1 to 3), he expresses his joy and thanks to God that the Thessalonians are true to Christ even in the face of persecution. He assures them how much he loves them and longs to see them. In answer to continued slanders that were being hurled at him at Thessalonica, as Timothy had no doubt told him, he recalls that all his actions there had been honorable and unselfish.

It seems strange that Paul was accused of flattery, greed, and pride (I Thess. 2: 5, 6). But in his day numerous preachers and teachers of every kind traveled about the Empire. Many were impostors, out to make a good living at the expense of gullible people. Some evidently thought, or pretended, that Paul was just another one of these frauds. Others, especially the Jews, attacked his message. They rejected and denounced his gospel concerning Jesus Christ. But the readers could answer this charge. They had found faith, hope, and love through Christ; they had gladly accepted the gospel Paul brought (I Thess. 1: 2-10). They knew that it was true and they knew that Paul was sincere. Apart from his thanks to God for them and his desire to see them, he had for them one great prayer: that they would grow in faith and "increase and abound in love to one another and to all men" (I Thess. 3: 9-13).

In the second part of the letter (I Thess., chs. 4; 5), Paul takes up problems that were troubling the church. This group of Christians had just come out of pagan life. They lacked Christian experience and training; they had no experienced leaders to guide them. Naturally questions arose as to how to live and worship. They may have sent word by Timothy that they wanted help in such matters. At any rate, when Paul heard what their difficulties were, he determined to help them in this letter.

They needed to be warned again to keep the highest standards in sex and family life (I Thess. 4: 1-8). Such sex morality was not a common pagan virtue. Many pagans lived pure lives, but there was much immorality. In some pagan religions this was not condemned; in a few it was actually approved on certain riotous occasions. The Jews had in the Old Testament strong teaching on moral purity, and the Christian message inherited it. Paul insisted that every Christian keep that high standard and avoid loose living. He also urged continued mutual love and faithful daily work (I Thess. 4: 9-12).

Another question concerned the end of the world. Good and evil are in conflict. Will God's purpose be realized? Will the right win out? For Paul and all who believed that Christ is the Lord of life, the answer was a confident yes. They hoped for the final triumph to come soon, and they knew that only the power of God would bring the victory.

But when some of the Thessalonian Christians died before the end came, the others raised a question. Would their loved ones who had died share in the coming victory? Would they take part in the return of Christ and the victory of his cause? Paul assured them that the dead would rise first. All Christians, the living and the dead, would share in the great final triumph (I Thess. 4: 13-18).

No one could know when the end would come. Paul expected it rather soon, and his converts shared his hope. He told them they must be ready. But he was too sensible to give way to excitement. He went about his Christian work, and he urged them to do the same. They must watch and be ready, but they must also be steadfast and patient. It was natural for them to look eagerly for the end. Persecuted as they were, the end of the age would bring deliverance, safety, and every Christian joy. But only if they stayed true to their faith and task. Paul shared this hope of Christ's coming and triumph, but he never let it keep him from doing well what he had to do for Christ (I Thess. 5: 1-22).

The Second Letter

One letter was not enough. The Thessalonians still had not understood the need for quiet, faithful Christian living. They were greatly impressed by Paul's words about watching for the coming of Christ and the end of the age. So much did they think of this that a report began to circulate among them that the final day was right at hand. Some had quit working, so certain were they that they no longer needed an income. They went about stirring up excitement. Since they no longer received wages, they became a burden on their fellow Christians, and they caused outsiders to scorn the gospel as a source of unrest.

What troubled Paul most of all was that these idle people claimed that a letter from him justified their action. They declared that according to his letter the end certainly was coming at once, so that they need no longer work. This they may have concluded from his first letter, in which he urged them to watch and be ready always for Christ's return. But he had also warned them "to live quietly, to mind your own affairs, and to work with your hands" (I Thess. 4: 11). So he suspected or was certain that someone had forged a letter in his name to say things he never had taught.

Obviously a second letter was needed, and he wrote it as soon as he heard of the situation; this was probably only a few months after the former one. First of all he thanked God that the Thessalonian Christians, though still persecuted for their faith, continued faithful and loyal. He assured them that God would give them a blessing that would make every hardship worth enduring (II Thess. 1: 3-12). Then he recalled that while still with them he had taught them that further events of opposition to God were to come before the end would arrive. So they should not be overeager, or think that the end had already come. Christ will come; his cause will triumph; but in God's own time (II Thess., ch. 2). With this assurance to steady them, and without restless worry, their Christian duty is to stand fast in faith and live each day a loyal, helpful life. Each one should work, earn his own living, and have means to help those who are in need through no fault of their own (II Thess., ch. 3).

To make sure that no forged letter could get a hearing,

Paul, after dictating the letter, added in his own handwriting the closing greeting and prayer for the readers (II Thess. 3: 17, 18). This would serve as his signature, by which his genuine letters could be identified.

Living in Christian Hope

Four great Christian convictions stand out in these two letters. First and foremost, Christians trust in God; they find in him the ground of their confidence. Their hope was not built on outward security; both Paul and the Thessalonians knew what persecution and trials meant. Nor could they trust in their own ability; they were not adequate to deal with this world and with death and the time to come. Their ground of confidence was that God, with his good will and power, was with them to see them through every trial and to bring them to final victory and fellowship in his Kingdom (I Thess. 5: 9, 23, 24; II Thess. 1: 11, 12; 2: 16, 17; 3: 3). God does not excuse the Christian from life's struggles. But to everyone who trusts him he gives the strength to endure them, the guidance and courage to choose the right, and the promise of full rescue at the end from all evil and trial.

So, in the second place, the Christian gospel is a message of hope. Because God is faithful, the Christian is safe if he puts his trust in his Father. He may face the uncertain future, not with despair, nor even with doubt, but with full confidence that his life is in the best of hands. He will be eager for the full coming of God's Kingdom, but, knowing that the victory of Christ is certain, he can be patient, serving the Church and helping his fellow men (I Thess. 1: 3, 4; 4: 13, 14; 5: 8-11).

Thus this trust in God yields the fruit of steadfastness. And this is a great achievement. It is not too hard to be brave and do the right for a brief time. But to hold steady and to continue on in the service of Christ day after day calls for great resources of strength. That strength is not in man; it is the gift of God and by God's power man may be steadfast. Even when persecuted, God's people can hold to their faith. Even when ridiculed, they can be glad in the faith they profess and do their part in the Christian fellowship they share (II Thess. 1: 3, 4; 3: 5).

Then, too, the wholesome place of work is clear from these letters, especially the second one. It sounds romantic to speak of the great day coming; it seems pious to go about and talk of the great privileges God will soon give. There is a place for such hope; the Christian looks confidently for the final victory of God's cause. But the Christian is not permitted to know when that will come. In the meantime, he is socially responsible; he is to think not only of caring for himself but also of providing for his family and for others who suffer disaster and need (I Thess. 4: 9-11; II Thess. 3: 6-13).

Thus honest work has a vital part in the Christian's life. It keeps him from being a busybody and nuisance; it makes him a self-respecting member of society; it enables him to be a helpful friend. Paul had worked to support himself while in Thessalonica (I Thess. 2: 9; II Thess. 3: 7-9). In that way he had given the Christians there an example of the dignity of work. In this as in so many things his deep faith and untiring service to the Church of Christ are united with a strong note of practical common sense.

Reading Hints: Notice how a prayer for the readers (I Thess. 3: 11-13; II Thess. 2: 16, 17) divides each letter into a longer first part and a shorter concluding part.

What charges against himself does Paul answer in these letters? How does he answer them? What difficulties and problems at Thessalonica does Paul mention?

Great Words on Christian Living: I Thess. 4: 9-12; 5: 12-22.

The main thing is to read these and all the other letters in full. If possible, read each one at one sitting. That is the way the people who first received them heard them read.

CHAPTER 10

The Letter to the Galatians

WHAT made Paul so important? In part it was the deep faith and untiring zeal he showed in everything he did. With his ability and his active earnestness he was bound to become a leader. While still an opponent of the Christians, he was "extremely zealous" (Gal. 1: 14) and led the persecution of the disciples. Once he had been converted, "immediately he proclaimed Jesus" (Acts 9: 20), and from then on he constantly used every opportunity to preach the gospel. Such intense, unceasing activity made him a marked man.

THE GOSPEL REACHES OUT TO GENTILES

But Paul is a world figure chiefly because of his outstanding work in preaching to the Gentiles. He was not the first Christian to do this. Even before he was converted, others were preparing the way for world-wide missionary work. Stephen saw that the Temple and the law of Moses were not the real way to salvation (Acts 6: 13, 14; 7: 48, 53). Philip preached to the Samaritans and the Ethiopians (Acts 8: 5-40). Peter, somewhat against his inclination, was led to preach to the Gentile Cornelius and his household (Acts, ch. 10). More daring still was the development at Antioch in Syria. There both Jews and Gentiles were won to Christ and they lived in one brotherhood without requiring the Gentiles to keep the Jewish rites. This occurred before Paul became part of the Antioch group; he came in later to help Barnabas (Acts 11: 19-26).

The Apostle to the Gentiles

Yet Paul preached more widely and won more Gentiles to Christ than did any other Christian of his day. First with Barnabas, and then as an independent pioneer, he went out on extensive preaching tours. Not that this was merely his personal plan. The Spirit of God led the Antioch leaders to send out for this work their two strongest "prophets and teachers," Barnabas and Saul (Acts 13: 1-3). Even when they started they did not know that the appeal to the Gentiles would be their greatest work. But in city after city, when the Jews stubbornly refused to believe the gospel, the Gentiles listened and accepted Christ. The preachers did not stop speaking to Jews. But when that failed, they turned also to Gentiles, and many of them believed.

Thus churches arose that were mainly Gentile. As we have seen, had these Gentiles at once adopted the Jewish law and practiced all the Jewish ceremonies, no Jew would have objected. But Paul and Barnabas had not required this. So some of the Jewish Christians began to ask, How can a Gentile become a true Christian without keeping the Jewish law and rites? Since Paul was the most effective preacher to the Gentiles, the attack centered on him. A crisis occurred when Jewish Christians came to Antioch in Syria and insisted that every Gentile believer in Christ must keep the Jewish law; every man must be circumcised (Acts 15: 1).

It was the Jerusalem conference, described in Chapter 8, which took up this problem. All of the apostles agreed that Gentile Christians need not keep the law's system of ceremonies. It appears, though Paul never mentions it, that in order not to offend Jewish Christians, the Gentile Christians were asked to keep certain rules, mainly food laws, just as Christians do not serve ham when they hold a joint meeting with Jews today. But the conference rejected the idea that Gentiles had to keep the Jewish rites in order to be saved. It may seem that the issue was fully settled (Acts 15:1-29).

Yet dispute continued. Those who insisted that all Christians must keep the law continued to oppose Paul. They followed him into the regions where he carried on his mission work, and the clash reached a climax in the Roman province of Galatia. There, in the center of Asia Minor, in the four cities of Antioch, Iconium, Lystra, and Derbe, Paul had founded churches on his first missionary journey (Acts, chs. 13; 14). Even then Jewish hostility to Paul had been strong; he was denounced, expelled, and even stoned. New Jewish Christians, zealous for the law, had come to Galatia in an attempt to destroy the influence of Paul and win the churches to their point of view.

The Attack Upon Paul

Why did these Christian Jews fight Paul? Obviously they found something in his message that clashed with Judaism as they had inherited it. If we can grasp what it was, we can understand his letter to the Galatian churches and what it means for us.

The bitter Jewish hostility proves that Paul had not required Gentiles to become full Jews in order to become Christians. When he preached the gospel, he asked the hearer, whether Jew or Gentile, to turn from all wrong, put full faith in Christ who had brought God's redemption to men, and live a life of trust in God and love to men. This man can do by the power that God's Spirit gives. Christian Jews might continue to practice Jewish rites—indeed, Paul often did—as long as it did not break up the fellowship of the Church. But Paul did not ask Gentiles to do so.

This was what Paul's opponents denounced. No doubt they were sincere, as Paul had been when he persecuted Christians before his conversion. They thought it their duty to stop what Paul was doing, and to show his converts how wrong he was. Just what did they tell the Galatians?

They made three main charges. One they aimed at Paul himself. They asserted that he was not a true apostle. He had not lived with Jesus in Galilee, nor gone to Jerusalem with him. He was not one of the Twelve. So he had no right to claim an independent position in the Church, nor was he the authority who could tell churches what the gospel is. For his message he had to depend on the original apostles. When he departed from their teaching and way of life, he was a traitor to the Christian cause. He must be disowned.

In addition to attacking Paul's authority, his opponents declared that his gospel was not the true gospel. In the Old Testament, God had given the law as an everlasting standard. No man could set it aside. It prescribed circumcision for every man of God's covenant people (Gen. 17: 9-14); it required observance of certain feasts and other ceremonies. To belong to God's people one must keep these laws. So every Christian must accept and observe them. It seems that at first the opponents did not demand all this; they started by getting the Galatians to observe the feasts (Gal. 4: 10); by the time Paul wrote they had gone on to insist on circumcision. But Paul saw that they were on the way to requiring the keeping of the entire law to be saved; they implied that to be a Christian one must do all it says. Since Paul had not required Gentiles to keep this law, his foes denounced him.

Their third attack was against the moral results of Paul's preaching. Judaism always stressed the necessity for right conduct, for obedience to God's will. Paul's opponents feared that unless the Jewish law regulated man's conduct, lax and immoral life would result. They held that the law was necessary to insure good living.

These three charges had alarming success. The Galatian Christians were impressed. They wanted to have the true gospel, and the zeal of Paul's opponents influenced them. They lacked experience and training, and began to yield to his foes. They began to observe the Jewish feasts; they could take joy in such festivals. They were about ready to adopt the rite of circumcision, because the law required it, and they were being told that to be saved they must do what the law says.

When Paul heard of their attitude, he knew that the Church faced a crisis. There are situations in which one man's action is decisive for the future progress of the Church, and this was such an occasion. The time was short. He had to write at once, to stop the drift of events. So at Corinth, about A.D. 51 or 52, or possibly at Ephesus some two years later, he wrote this urgent and vital letter.

Paul's Fighting Reply

From the first line Paul strikes at the false teaching of his opponents. In writing to the Thessalonians he had simply named the writers at the beginning, but here, to answer his opponents at once, he says that he *is* an apostle, divinely appointed. The Christians who are with him agree with what he has to say, so he names them as coauthors. When he prays that the readers may receive the Christian blessings of divine grace and peace, he points out that men cannot earn these blessings by keeping the law; they are God's gift to sinners; through Christ's death God has saved us from this evil age. The opening thus defends his apostleship and points out how Christians are really saved (Gal. 1: 1-5).

Instead of the usual thanksgiving and praise, Paul bluntly rebukes the Galatians for their readiness to give up the true Christian faith (Gal. 1: 6-10). He warns them sternly that such surrender will bring ruin upon them. It is fatal to go back on the truth.

Paul then turns to the three charges against him. To show that he has his gospel from Christ, and is a true and faithful apostle, he traces step by step the story of his life (Gal. 1: 11 to 2: 21). Though he had been a persecutor, God had converted him, contrary to what he had deserved. He at once began to preach the gospel; he did not wait for the Twelve to teach or approve him; and his work had divine approval in its results. Even in Judea, Christians learned of his work and thanked God for him. When a dispute about receiving Gentiles into the Church arose, the Jerusalem apostles approved his gospel. When at Syrian Antioch, Peter and Barnabas wavered and for the sake of Jewish food laws split the Church there, Paul stood firm. He pointed out to Peter that Jews and Gentiles alike have failed and so depend on God's grace; hence it is wrong to ask the Gentiles to keep a law which the Jews themselves have not been able to keep.

Thus the defense of his apostleship leads on to the defense of his gospel, and he vigorously states his position (Gal., chs. 3; 4). Every person fails; he sins. This is the basis of Paul's thinking about the way of salvation. If we had to earn our salvation by first doing what the law demands, we should all be lost, because we all sin. So all men, of all races, share a common need, and the law cannot meet it. The law promises blessings to those who keep God's covenant, who do his will. But since men do wrong, they cannot claim those blessings. Men know that they should do God's will, but if honest they know that they fail to do so. The law alone leads to despair.

That is why Paul so strongly resisted the demand that the Galatians should keep the feasts and be circumcised. Why were they being asked to do these things? Because the law requires them, and to have God's favor one must keep the law; so Paul's opponents said. But right here is the difficulty; man finds that he cannot do all that the law prescribes. He may do many things that it demands, but he knows that his thoughts, words, and acts are no so clean, honest, and helpful as they should be.

So some other way is needed. And this is just what the gospel offers. To men who fail, who cannot be saved by the law, God in his goodness offers the way to forgiveness, to fellowship with him, to new life. He asks man to regret his failure, to put his faith fully and sincerely in Christ, and to live in Christian love by the power of God's Spirit. To insist upon keeping the law not only demands the impossible, but also obscures the fact that God saves through Christ, and that even in the Old Testament God points to the way of faith as the path of man's hope (Gal. 3: 6-9).

The need is universal. The way of faith and love offers a way of salvation independent of race or Jewish ritual. This is the universal gospel, freely offered to Jew and Gentile alike. It leaves no room for distinctions of race or for any claim that man can save himself by what he does.

Yet, as Paul says in answer to the third charge, this new life of faith and love is a life of moral vigor (Gal. 5: 1 to 6: 10). A set of laws will not solve man's moral problem. He has to be right inside. He has to be free from evil desire and habits; he has to have a heart set on the good; he has to be led by a spirit of love. The life of faith gives just what man needs. "Faith working through love" is Paul's picture of the Christian life (Gal. 5: 6). This life has real freedom—freedom from mere rules and from the grip of sin and evil. It has real love—sincere good will for others. It is a life of power, for God's Spirit is its strength. So "the fruit of the Spirit is love, joy, peace, patience, kindness, goodness, faithfulness, gentleness, self-control" (Gal. 5: 22, 23).

While Luke in The Acts tells nothing of the trouble in Galatia, the facts that the letter was preserved, and that the churches there survived, indicate that the letter came in time and with such power that it led the Galatians to agree with Paul. Evidently Paul had considerable confidence that this would be the result. When, after dictating the letter, he takes up the pen to add the conclusion (Gal. 6: 11-18), he sums up his position in calmer tones. Though still stern, he speaks as if he expects his words to be heard with respect. But the fact that no other letter of Paul has so long a summary shows how important he thought the issue was and how determined he was to save the Galatians from a fatal mistake.

The Lasting Message

Paul wrote in a specific ancient situation, and some things he says are hard to understand. But this letter states the central Christian faith with such power that at crucial times in the Church this letter has had great influence. At the Reformation, for example, it was a source of light and direction for Luther, Calvin, and other Christians who were seeking the heart of the gospel.

The letter speaks the message of grace. Man's hope is not in himself but in God. In Jesus Christ God has fully supplied man's need; he forgives and restores the man who turns to him; he constantly gives the believer help and power to live in fellowship with God and in brotherhood with other men.

Therefore the letter speaks the message of faith. From men who cannot meet their own needs God wants an honest and willing response of faith. This is not merely belief, though it includes that. It is the acceptance of God's grace in gratitude; it is the trusting of life to the God who has made himself known in Christ. It is the giving of the whole life in grateful trust and obedience to the God who has given man everything he needs.

The letter also speaks the message of freedom. But note what this means. Freedom is not the privilege to do as you please, or perhaps to do nothing. Man is not free when he is a slave of sin and evil habits. When Christ sets him free (Gal. 5: 1), he is free from guilt, from sin, from bondage to rules and rites; he is free to do right. This is the great freedom which the gospel offers—freedom to do willingly and well what is right. It is not man's achievement; it is God's gift and it is due to God's power. But it is the real freedom.

Thus the letter speaks the message of moral power. Such power never comes by making a law and telling man what he must do. There is a place for law; it states man's duty and shows him the right way. But what man needs is not only the inner freedom we mentioned but also the power to do the right. Real faith, which gives the whole life to God, opens to men the source of power to live as they should. The Spirit of God will uphold the sincere, wholehearted believer in a life that is Christlike and true.

And so the letter speaks a message of hope to every man. This is a universal gospel. It reaches as far as human need. God will forgive and help every man, of whatever race or past, if he will really turn from his wrong and gratefully accept what God offers. "There is neither Jew nor Greek, there is neither slave nor free, there is neither male nor female; for you are all one in Christ Jesus" (Gal. 3: 28).

This is the gospel for all men on equal terms. In the providence of God it came first to the Jews, but it was meant for all men everywhere. It was Paul who saw this so clearly and defended it so effectively that we have it today as the gospel for the world. When the crisis arose in Galatia, God had a man ready to see and state the issue, and to lead the Church to hold fast to the central gospel of "faith working through love" (Gal. 5: 6).

READING HINTS: By all means read this letter at one sitting. Note how earnestly Paul argues his case, and how he sums it up at the end in Gal. 6: 11-18.

These passages are important in showing Paul's position: Gal. 1: 3-5; 1: 11, 12; 2: 15, 16, 20; 3: 9, 26-28; 5: 1, 13, 14, 22-26; 6: 2, 7-10, 14.

CHAPTER 11

"First Corinthians"

"To live like a Corinthian" was the way the ancients described loose and immoral conduct. Another common saying, that it was not for every man to go to Corinth, meant that temptation there was certain to drag many visitors down into sin. What could the gospel do for Corinth?

Certainly Paul could not neglect this busy city. Corinth was one of the largest centers of trade and travel in the Roman Empire. It stood at the south end of the Isthmus of Corinth, a four-mile-wide strip which was the land bridge for traffic between the northern and southern parts of Greece. To avoid the dangerous stormy capes at the south tip of Greece, traders often unloaded ships on one side of the isthmus, carried the goods across, and reloaded them in another ship on the other side. Small seagoing ships were even hauled across the isthmus on a wooden causeway. Nero tried to build a canal across this neck of land at the very place where, nearly sixty years ago, modern engineers actually completed a canal for ocean ships. He failed, but trade moved across the isthmus just the same.

In this active center were found not only Greeks but also numerous visitors from many countries and races. Some settled down to live there. Many stayed but a short time, and the transient traders, the thrill-hunting tourists, and the money-seeking natives all did their part to lower the moral tone of the city.

Corinth was also the capital of the Roman province of Achaia, the name then applied to Greece. From his residence in this city the Roman proconsul, appointed by the Roman senate, ruled the province.

Paul Brings the Gospel to Corinth

It was on his second great missionary journey that Paul came to Corinth, and stopped there for the longest stay he made anywhere on that journey. At Athens, which he had just left, he had had little success, although some became believers even there (Acts 17: 34). He came to Corinth with inward misgivings (I Cor. 2: 3), but he had been sent by God to preach the gospel, so he preached it. At first he was alone in this work, for Silas and Timothy, his helpers, were in Macedonia revisiting the churches founded shortly before.

Paul found lodging with a Christian couple of Jewish descent. Aquila and Priscilla had been forced to leave Rome and had just come to Corinth. They were tentmakers. So was Paul; by this trade he supported himself except when gifts came from friends to help him. He made friends with Aquila and Priscilla, and with them worked at his trade. Part of his time he spent in preaching. When Silas and Timothy came from Macedonia, they brought gifts from the Christians there (II Cor. 11: 9); this no doubt left Paul free to spend more time in preaching Christ (Acts 18: 1-4).

As usual, he began by preaching in the synagogue services, where the leaders allowed visiting Jews to speak. The Jews soon saw that the new faith would require them to rebuild their life around Christ as Lord, and would break the strict barrier between Jew and Gentile. Some believed, but since most of them strenuously opposed Paul, he and his converts withdrew from the synagogue, and he continued his preaching in the home of a Gentile, Titus Justus, who lived next door. There Paul carried on his work for eighteen months (Acts 18: 5-11), and won many Jews and Gentiles.

Finally the hostile Jews saw a chance to act against him. A change of governors had occurred: Gallio became proconsul, about A.D. 51. The Jews brought Paul before him and charged Paul with spreading an illegal religion; the Empire permitted only officially recognized religions to be preached. The Christian faith, so Paul and the Christians said, was the true faith of Israel, now brought to its full form in Jesus Christ and the Church. But the Jews hotly denied that the Christians were true Jews, and declared that since Paul's faith was not a recognized religion, the governor should ban it. Gallio sensed the vital link between Paul's gospel and the ancestral faith of the Jews, and refused to act against him (Acts 18: 12-17). Paul thus could continue to preach.

This mission in Corinth had wide effect. Not only at Corinth, but in neighboring regions too, the Church spread. At Cenchreae, the eastern port of Corinth, a church arose (Rom. 16: 1). In addition, when Paul speaks of "all the saints who are in the whole of Achaia" (II Cor. 1: 1), he implies that the gospel had spread widely from Corinth, by conversion of visitors to Corinth and by the preaching his helpers did in smaller places.

Paul's chief task was to seek out new places to preach. So when the church seemed well established at Corinth, he left. After a visit to Jerusalem and Antioch in Syria, he struck out on a third mission tour, and soon came to Ephesus for the longest stay he made on any of his three main journeys. During this time the eloquent Apollos came to Corinth and won many followers (Acts 18: 18 to 19: 1). Possibly Peter also came there, for he later had supporters in Corinth.

The Lost Letter

Paul was too wise to leave his young churches without friendship and counsel. He soon wrote a letter to Corinth. It is lost, unless, as some suppose, parts of it, now inserted in later letters, survive in I Cor. 6: 12-20 and II Cor. 6: 14 to 7: 1.

Paul plainly refers to it in I Cor. 5: 9. The letter insisted that Christians, completely dedicated to Christ, are to live lives clean in thought and act. They are not to have fellowship in the Church with those who persist in immoral living.

Corinth was known for its loose sex standards, and some of the converts found it hard to break with such low ways of life. And either because they wanted to misunderstand him, or because he had not made himself perfectly clear, they twisted his words. They took him to mean that they must never have anything to do with any person who lives an immoral life. They said that this would force them out of all social and community life; in Corinth, to engage in business or any civic activity would force a Christian to deal with immoral people. From this reply, we clearly see how widespread moral rottenness was in the city as a whole. But what Paul insisted was that the Christians must not permit any of their church group to continue in such sinful living. If anyone persisted in immorality, the others were to expel him until he repented.

Why Paul Wrote "First Corinthians"

Several things soon led Paul to write again. He had to correct the misunderstanding of his earlier letter. Also, members of Chloe's household came telling of party divisions in the church at Corinth. We do not know exactly who Chloe was. She was a Christian, of Corinth or Ephesus; probably she was engaged in some business that required travel by members of her household. Still other messengers came. Stephanas, Paul's first convert in Greece (I Cor. 16: 15), arrived with Fortunatus and Achaicus to visit Paul and give him news. One of these groups also handed Paul a letter from Corinth. I Cor. 7: 1 mentions it, and the repeating of the same introductory words, "Now concerning," in I Cor. 7: 25; 8: 1; 12: 1; 16: 1, suggests that the letter raised all the questions these verses mention.

The situation that this letter and the oral reports revealed called for prompt and skillful attention. So, at the end of A.D. 56 or early in 57, Paul wrote his second letter to Corinth. Since the earlier one is lost, we call this second one First Corinthians. Why is it still worth reading? Chiefly because Paul always deals with problems in the light of the eternal gospel. He does not evade or compromise to avoid facing an issue; he tries to find what the Christian faith means in the daily life of the church he wants to help.

In this case, Paul has to rebuke and correct the church on several points. But he does not begin with rebuke. He has the insight to see that beneath the failures and faults of these people lie real faith and great possibilities. First of all, he thanks God that divine grace has come to them, renewed their lives, and given them so many splendid gifts. He assures them that God will continue to uphold them; they can count on God and need never despair, even if at times they fail and require correction (I Cor. 1: 4-9).

The Sin of a Divided Church

A major problem was the party divisions that were damaging both brotherhood and Christian character (I Cor. 1: 10 to 4: 21). Apparently four separate groups had been formed, each claiming a great leader. One boasted that they followed Paul, another stood by Apollos, a third proudly supported Cephas (Peter). Still a fourth scorned all human leaders and claimed that Christ belonged to *them*. All four groups were narrow and divisive. The lack of a church building may have aided such dissension. Small groups had to meet in homes, and those who thought alike would tend to meet together and feel separate from the other disciples.

For Paul such division was intolerable. Christ alone is the head of the Church. To praise one human leader and have no use for others is not Christian. All Christians are to rejoice in the gifts of all leaders, and profit by what all can give. "So let no one boast of men. For all things are yours, whether Paul or Apollos or Cephas . . . , all are yours; and you are Christ's; and Christ is God's" (I Cor. 3: 21-23). Paul rightly rebukes those who try to make a party leader of him. He has no more right to the final loyalty of Christians than does Apollos or Cephas. They all are servants of Christ.

Christian Marriage

This church also had problems of sex and family life. One member had married or was living with his father's wife; probably she was his stepmother (I Cor., ch. 5). To Paul this was more serious because the Church, used to lax standards in Corinth and to the breaking up of homes, had not condemned the wrong. Other Christians were tempted to think, as so many pagans did, that lawless sex relations did not hurt the spiritual life (I Cor. 6: 12-20). Still others took the opposite view. They feared that marriage could not be approved, and that to continue unmarried was to live a purer life than those did who married and raised a family (I Cor., ch. 7).

Paul knew that body, mind, and spirit unite to make one life. To abuse the body or live an impure life harms man's spiritual life and mental health; it also injures and corrupts society. Some persons can live pure and wholesome lives without marriage, and so can do special work in life which married people cannot well undertake. For most people marriage is normal and best. But Paul saw dangers in it. Married couples may think so much of the rights and duties of the home that they fail to serve Christ in the church and community. Indeed, Paul, thinking that the world would not last much longer (I Cor. 7: 29-31), held that Christians who could might well avoid marriage and be free to live only for Christ in the last troubled days of the world.

Christian readers today may well feel that Paul did not see the full truth when he asserted that marriage, though quite all right for a Christian, is a second best. He himself spoke with considerable restraint upon this subject (I Cor. 7: 25,

40). In any case, he saw clearly that God made man for marriage and that it was not sinful to marry. He saw that most Christians should marry. He insisted that marriage is a permanent union between one man and one woman; in this he echoed Jesus' teaching (I Cor. 7: 10). Unmarried people are to live clean lives of self-control. Married people are to be faithful and loyal to their life partners. These standards are a Christian obligation: "Your body is a temple of the Holy Spirit which is in you . . . : glorify God therefore in your body" (I Cor. 6: 19, 20).

How to Live with Pagans

Paul had learned with regret that some Christians, having personal quarrels, had gone to court over business matters (I Cor. 6: 1-11). By doing so they brought shame on the Church in the community. Paul felt that they should let Christians rather than pagan courts settle their disputes, and that Christians should be ready to accept injustice rather than bring disgrace upon Christ and the Church. He was concerned for the spiritual life of the Christians, for the reputation of the Church, and for its witness to men outside. From all these points of view quarrels and lawsuits did great harm.

How far can the Christian share life with non-Christians? In business, government, and social life some contacts are unavoidable. But in Corinth pagan life was marked by idolatry and polytheism. A pagan home had its gods; so did a city, a labor union or guild, and the many social groups. What, the church asks Paul, are we to do, especially about eating food sacrificed to idols? Can we share meals in pagan homes? (See I Cor. 8: 1 to 11: 1.)

Paul at once states an important point: Think what influence your action will have on others, especially on weak fellow Christians. You may know there is only one God; to eat meat offered to an idol would not hurt your faith. But a fellow Christian of weak conscience may feel that by your act you share in idolatry, and if your example leads him to eat against his conscience, you hurt your brother by what you do. It is better to avoid eating such meat than to damage or ruin your brother's Christian faith.

To enforce this truth, Paul points out (I Cor., ch. 9) that as an apostle he has many rights that he has not used. He has gladly given them up in order to serve Christ and the Church as fully as possible. For the Christian way is not to think first of one's own rights; it is the cause of Christ and the welfare of others that count.

Moreover, even those who think they are strong in the faith may well be careful. They think that to go to a pagan feast will not hurt them. But there are evil powers in pagan circles that are at work to capture the lives of all who live there. The Christian does everything to the honor of God and Christ. He wants to win as many as possible to share his faith. But he cannot take over the standards and pleasures of the world. So Paul warns the Corinthians that they must not share and approve customs and rites that contradict the Christian faith.

Christian Worship

When Paul takes up disorders that happened in meetings for worship, he gives one instruction that seems rather strange to us. He insists that for a woman to pray with head unveiled is disgraceful (I Cor. 11: 2-16). This he said with three things in mind. He accepted the Old Testament teaching that God had given the leading role to the man, and the woman's hat or veil served as a sign of this. He saw that man and woman do not have the same role in life, and he thought dress should reflect this difference. He also knew that modest women of good character did not parade their physical charms in public in that day; had Christian women gone unveiled to Christian meetings for worship, they would have been suspected of immoral practices. Paul did not want that to happen.

A more serious trouble at Corinth was the confusion, selfishness, and even drunkenness that marred the Lord's Supper (I Cor. 11: 17-34). Each person or group brought food, for the Supper was a hunger-satifying meal, eaten with the memory of the death of Christ. But some ate all they wanted, and even drank too much wine, while their poorer fellows were still hungry. This was neither reverent nor brotherly. Paul urges them, in the words we still use today in our Communion service, that together they should gratefully recall the meaning Jesus put into his last supper with his disciples. As a practical suggestion, he advises the readers, if they are very hungry, to eat something before they come to the common meal. At the Lord's Supper they should all join reverently in remembering the benefits of the death of Christ for his followers.

Still another source of confusion in worship was the egotistical use of spiritual gifts (I Cor., chs. 12 to 14). The Church had received the Holy Spirit to guide its worship and life, and each person had been given some gift with which to serve his Lord and his Church. But too many had used their gifts to make a mere display and gain credit in the eyes of others. Of the many gifts (I Cor. 12: 28), two were much discussed. Some people spoke with tongues—an unintelligible, highly emotional speech. Others prophesied with great earnestness. Which was the better gift?

Paul's answer showed both sympathy and common sense. First of all, the Spirit will lead men to praise and honor Christ; an emotional outburst which fails to do that is not inspired by the Spirit of God. Just as the body has many members which work together to form one body, so the Church has many members with varying gifts; all are needed and should be honored. To go to the heart of the matter, the greatest gift is Christian love—intelligent, friendly, patient, sacrificial good will—and all gifts must be used in the spirit of love. Since the purpose of these gifts is to help others, the gift of prophecy, which speaks so that others can understand, is greater than the gift of speaking with tongues. Not spectacular show, but whether it serves the Church and helps fellow Christians, is the test of each special gift (I Cor. 14: 26). In worship Christians should be orderly and think of each other. "God is not a God of confusion but of peace" (I Cor. 14: 33).

The Resurrection Hope

Some Christians in Corinth denied Paul's teaching of the resurrection of the dead. The spirit of man, they agreed, would be saved. But to them the body was a burden, and they saw no place for it in the future life. In his answer (I Cor., ch. 15), Paul first recalls the resurrection of Jesus. This is our earliest written record of that event, for the Gospels were written later than this letter. Paul then goes on to argue that we too shall be raised. But not to have the same body we now have. It will be a new body, a spiritual body.

Evidently Paul wants to say three things. First, the body is now a part of man and so a part of the Christian life; if this is denied, immorality is encouraged. Then, too, in the future life man will be a complete person, and not a pale shadow or fragment of himself. Finally, the body he then will have will be free from all the imperfections of this present one. The main thing is that the Christian will be with God and Christ, in a full life that will give fellowship, security, and happiness in the perfect Kingdom of God.

In this faith Christians can go ahead with their work. One thing the Corinthians were to do was to take a collection for the destitute Christians in Jerusalem (I Cor. 16: 1-4). Thus this collection was not for their own use. Paul was teaching them to give for others and to think of the world Church. Then, after giving other instructions and greetings (I Cor. 16: 5-20), he concluded the letter with a final Christian message in his own handwriting (I Cor. 16: 21-24).

The Gospel for Corinth—and for Us

Great Christian convictions stand out clearly in this letter:

The gospel has the power to change sinful men; even in wicked Corinth, Christ proved able to save them.

The Christian should make a clean break with evil living. Christian living dedicates to God the body as well as the mind and heart and will.

God can use in his Church all people, no matter what their gifts. But since Christ saves men and meets their needs, they have no place for pride and personal display, but only for gratitude and loyalty to him. No human leader can take the place of authority; that belongs to Christ alone. The Christian must so act that others see what God's grace and power can do in a loyal disciple.

The Church is one Church. In it quarrels and divisions are shameful; Christ, the one Lord of the Church, binds all Christians together in one fellowship. So not only reverence toward God and gratitude for what Christ has done, but also good will for fellow Christians and readiness to use one's gifts to help them, are essential to true worship. The gift of the Holy Spirit and the resulting gift of Christian love must govern the way Christians use their special gifts in worship and life.

The Christian hope for the future gives the disciple every reason for joy and courage. All who put their faith in Jesus as Lord and prove faithful to him will share final victory with God and Christ. But the basis of human hope and confidence is not in man, but in God. In fact, as we look at the faults of the Corinthians, we know, as did Paul, that God's grace and power are the one solid basis of Christian hope.

READING HINTS: As you read, pay special attention to these great passages: Christ the power and wisdom of God (I Cor. 1: 17-31); the Holy Spirit gives man this truth and power (I Cor., ch. 2); the right attitude to human leaders (I Cor. 3: 5-10, 21-23); the Christian lives a clean physical life (I Cor. 6: 19, 20); how Paul looks at his own work (I Cor. 3: 5-11; ch. 9); the right way to eat the Lord's Supper (I Cor. 11: 17-34); Christian love—indispensable, Christlike, enduring (I Cor., ch. 13); the resurrection of Christ and the promise of our resurrection (I Cor., ch. 15).

CHAPTER 12

"Second Corinthians"

WHAT HAPPENED when Paul's messenger arrived at Corinth and delivered "First Corinthians" to the church? The Christians met together and heard the letter read; of that we may be certain. But what did they say and think of the letter? If we turn to the book of The Acts, we find no answer to our question. It never even says that Paul wrote letters to his churches. Nor does it tell us anything of the two greatest crises of which those letters speak, the attempt of some narrow Jewish Christians to win the Galatian churches away from Paul, and the rebellion against Paul at Corinth. Luke's purpose was to report the spread of the gospel; he tells how Paul came to each new place, how he began his work, and how he came to leave. He does not stop to describe the progress of each local church.

So we must piece together from Paul's own letters the story of later happenings at Corinth. And this we can do well enough to trace an exciting, but sometimes saddening, course of events. As we follow the account, we shall discover that what we call Second Corinthians may contain parts of various letters, which we shall come to know as "the lost letter," "the stern letter," and "the thankful letter."

New Attacks Upon Paul

When Paul wrote "First Corinthians" from Ephesus he hoped and prayed that the letter would correct the faults at

Corinth and establish harmony there. No doubt his words did much to improve conditions. But one great difficulty remained, and even grew worse. The Church had already split into parties, and this led hostile groups to oppose Paul himself (I Cor. 1: 12). Neither his letter nor the visit of Timothy, if he reached Corinth (I Cor. 4: 17; 16: 10), corrected this rebellious spirit.

The revolt was soon fanned into flame. Traveling teachers arrived who claimed to be apostles. Who they were we do not know; they were not members of the Twelve. But they were arrogant and clever in undermining Paul's influence, and they boasted of their Jewish ancestry and right to teach (II Cor. 11: 4, 5, 13, 20, 22). Under their influence, one Corinthian Christian became especially bitter against Paul, and led a determined movement to have nothing more to do with the apostle. Evidently this man's real fault was his personal pride and rebellious spirit, rather than any dangerous new teaching; later, when he had been punished and was sorry for his wrong, Paul was eager to see him forgiven and restored to full membership in the church (II Cor. 2: 5-8). But for a time the hostile intruders and the local rebel leader so upset the Corinthians that as a group they turned against Paul and repudiated his leadership.

Faced with this crisis, in the first half of A.D. 57, Paul made a quick trip across the Aegean Sea to Corinth. This seems clear from II Cor. 2: 1; 12: 14; 13: 1, 2, in which Paul speaks of a recent painful visit. He hoped that a personal visit would make the Corinthians see that he was doing the work of Christ and that they were wrong in following ambitious troublemakers. But he failed. The church rebuffed him. Since, then, he could do nothing at that time, he returned to Ephesus, after warning them that he would return on his way to Macedonia (II Cor. 1: 16). Before the time of that next visit, he hoped, they would have seen their mistake and decided to renew their loyalty to him.

The Stern Letter

But Paul did not leave the outcome merely to the passing of time. Twice before, he had written to Corinth—once in "First Corinthians," and still earlier in the so-called "lost letter." Now back in Ephesus, he wrote a third letter to Corinth. He refers to it in II Cor. 2: 4, 9; 7: 8. With deep sorrow, but with stern determination and blunt speech, he tried to bring the Corinthians to their senses and win back their friendship and trust. It is possible, as we shall see, that part of this "stern letter" survives in II Cor., chs. 10 to 13, where we find vigorous self-defense and sharp attack upon false leaders.

This stern letter Paul sent to Corinth by Titus. Not only was Titus to deliver the letter, but undoubtedly he was also to use personal persuasion to help the church. For its own health and growth it must disown the rebel leaders, change its attitude, and renew friendly relations with Paul. Since Paul expected to leave Ephesus soon, he arranged with Titus to meet him somewhere on the way in northern Asia Minor or in Macedonia.

Thus Paul left Ephesus, and found that in Troas "a door was opened" for him; people were ready to hear the gospel and believe. But his concern for Corinth left him no inner peace. He had to hear as soon as possible whether the stern letter and the appeal of Titus had won back the Corinthians. So he left Troas, and crossed over to Macedonia (II Cor. 2: 12, 13).

Finally, perhaps at Philippi, he met Titus, in the summer or fall of A.D. 57. The news was good. The church at Corinth had completely changed its attitude. It had disciplined the rebel leader and eagerly desired Paul's friendship. With deep relief and overflowing joy, the apostle promptly wrote a thankful letter to express his gratitude to God and his love for the Corinthians.

The Thankful Letter

The intense relief and thankful joy with which Paul writes this "thankful letter" come out again and again. At the start they find strong expression; his satisfaction that things are now right again in Corinth is increased as he remembers a miraculous escape from death that he recently has had in Asia, the Roman province in western Asia Minor (II Cor. 1: 3-11). This hardly refers to his grief over the trouble in Corinth, or even to the failure of the Ephesus mob to find him at the time of their riot (Acts 19: 23-41). That riot brought Paul into no real danger, and it caused him no despair, for he even wanted to go and speak to the mob. So the danger must have been one that he met while traveling in western Asia Minor. What it was we cannot know, but of one thing he was certain: God had delivered him from death, just as God had given him comfort by recent events at Corinth.

Paul's Ministry for Christ

Anxious to strengthen the loyalty of the Corinthians to him, Paul recalls what he has done. In everything he has been sincere with them (II Cor. 1: 12-14). He had a reason for not visiting them before going into Macedonia; he decided it would be better to give them time to change their attitude, so that his next visit could be a happy one. Instead of a prompt visit, he had written the stern letter to improve the situation (II Cor. 1: 15 to 2: 4). And his plan had worked; the church had repented and punished the rebel leader, so that Paul now can urge them to forgive the wrongdoer (II Cor. 2: 5-11).

Paul then starts to speak of his joy at getting the good news from Titus (II Cor. 2: 12, 13). But he breaks off—to resume the story only in II Cor. 7: 5—and thanks God for using him in the ministry. This leads him to describe at length the work and message of the apostolic minister (II Cor. 2: 14 to 6: 10). Only in God's power has he been able to do his work. The credit is not due to Paul, but he has been faithful (II Cor. 2: 14-17). He does not need to recommend himself; the faith and changed lives of the Corinthians are his letter of recommendation (II Cor. 3: 1-3). He is a minister in the new covenant which Christ has established; in it Christ is the Lord and God's Spirit is the life-giving power (II Cor. 3: 4-18).

The apostle is only a weak and mortal servant of Christ and the Church. Yet in him the renewing power of God is at work to give life to others and also to give eternal life to Paul (II Cor., ch. 4). Even death will not bring defeat or damage to Paul; God's Spirit is in him, and this is God's pledge that Paul will be at home with his Lord in the life to come. Spurred on by this promise, he makes every effort so to live that Christ will accept him at the final judgment (II Cor. 5: 1-10). Both reverent fear of his Lord and the powerful love of Christ spur him on in a faithful ministry of reconciliation. The heart of his gospel is that "God was in Christ reconciling the world to himself, not counting their trespasses against them, and entrusting to us the message of reconciliation" (II Cor. 5: 11-19). So, with earnest and undaunted zeal, Paul as an ambassador for Christ appeals to men and continues his work regardless of difficulty and danger (II Cor. 5: 20 to 6: 10).

Turning now to the church, Paul appeals strongly to them to respond to his love with a like affection (II Cor. 6: 11 to 7: 4). In the midst of this appeal is a warning against pagan ties that lead to sin in body and spirit (II Cor. 6: 14 to 7: 1). This warning, some have thought, may be a part of the "lost letter" mentioned in I Cor. 5: 9, which warned not to let immoral people stay in the church; or Paul includes it here because he knew there was constant temptation to immoral living in Corinth. But the main point in this section is the appeal to the readers to show to him the same affection he feels and has expressed for them.

Only now does Paul finally tell of his meeting with Titus, and of his joy and the joy of Titus at the good news from

Corinth. How happy the news made Paul it is easy to understand (II Cor. 7: 5-16).

Christian Giving

Grateful and loyal Christians have their tasks to do. For a time the Corinthians had neglected one of theirs. They had started a collection for the destitute Christians in Jerusalem, but then, disturbed by rebellion, had stopped. In II Cor., chs. 8 and 9, Paul urges them to resume this work, and complete it with a liberal offering before he comes.

With many arguments and appeals Paul works to make sure that they prepare a large gift. They must do as well as the neighboring churches (II Cor. 8: 1-5). Their gift will show their loyalty to Paul, for in this collection he has great interest (II Cor. 8: 7). They should give according to their ability (II Cor. 8: 10-12). To encourage them, Paul is sending to them Titus, whom they already know, and two other experienced helpers; he testifies to their integrity and zeal (II Cor. 8: 16-24).

They have promised to send a gift, and have started on it; now they must finish what they have begun. He has been telling others to count on Corinth, he has even said that the Corinthian gift is ready, and they must get the collection ready at once so that he and they will not be put to shame by his confidence in them (II Cor. 9: 1-5). It is cheerful giving that is real giving, and God will richly bless it (II Cor. 9: 6-11). Those who receive the gift will thank God for the faith and helpfulness of the Corinthians (II Cor. 9: 12-14). Let the Corinthians remember how great is God's gift to them in Christ, and then they surely will be ready to do all they can for those of Christ's people who are in need (II Cor. 8: 9; 9: 15). Thus Paul works to bind the Jewish and Gentile Christians together in good will and understanding; as one group gladly gives and the other gratefully receives, they will be drawn closer together in Christian love and trust.

A Stern Rebuke

Paul has said how glad he is at the renewed loyalty of the Corinthians. He has urged them to complete the collection. But now, surprisingly enough, come four chapters full of self-defense, attack, and warning (II Cor. 10: 1 to 13: 10). They denounce the Corinthians for sin and rebellion; they warn that Paul on his next visit will be as severe as necessary.

These chapters tell us many things about Paul. He concedes that his physical appearance and speaking ability are not impressive (II Cor. 10: 10). His method of work is to go to places where others have not preached, and establish new churches (II Cor. 10: 15, 16). He often supported himself (Acts 18: 3), and never accepted support from the city where he was working (II Cor. 11: 7-11); this was to avoid any suspicion that his interest was in money. His faithfulness and devotion to Christ are clear from the list of persecutions, hardships, and sufferings he endured (II Cor. 11: 23-29). He could boast of God-given visions, but they are no reason for personal pride. Indeed, to keep him humble, God has given him some trying physical "thorn" or ailment. But God has also given him the strength to bear it and to do his work (II Cor. 12: 1-10). God has even given him the power to work miracles among the Corinthians (II Cor. 12: 12). Knowing these things, the Corinthians should repent and show a new attitude before he comes again (II Cor. 12: 14 to 13: 10).

This outburst of defense and rebuke is amazing in its present position. In the preceding chapters Paul has described the Corinthians as repentant and obedient; he has spoken with thankful joy of the "perfect confidence" he has in them (II Cor. 7: 16). Why does he now denounce them so bitterly? Is he now attacking a still rebellious minority? Not a word suggests this; Paul is rebuking the entire church at Corinth.

This is exactly the way the Corinthians were acting when Paul wrote the stern letter from Ephesus, but it is not how things stood when Paul wrote the thankful letter from Macedonia. So even though these last four chapters do not include the demand for the punishment of the rebel leader at Corinth —a demand we know was in the stern letter (II Cor. 2: 9; 7: 12)—it looks as if these last four chapters were part of that stern letter, and were later inserted here because they told so much of Paul's message and ministry.

Paul's love and deep personal interest have been back of all that he has written in his letters to Corinth. He gives it a final expression in the closing instructions and greetings (II Cor. 13: 11-13), and ends with a prayer. "The grace of the Lord Jesus Christ and the love of God and the fellowship of the Holy Spirit be with you all" (II Cor. 13: 14).

The Last Visit to Corinth

From Macedonia, Paul went on to Greece for a stay of three months (Acts 20: 1-3). Probably he spent the winter there before going to Jerusalem with the offering from Corinth and other churches. Much of this time he no doubt spent with the Corinthians, who evidently completed their collection (Rom. 15: 26). Out of their time of confusion had come letters of Paul that show his pastoral heart, his faithfulness, and his deep understanding of his God-given gospel and ministry.

Reading Hints: Keep in mind the main outline:

I. Recent Events and Paul's Joy at Their Happy Outcome. Here II Cor. 1: 1 to 2: 13 and II Cor. 6: 11 to 7: 16 review the past, show Paul's honest love for the Corinthians, and express his joy at their renewed loyalty. II Cor. 2: 14 to 6: 10 are a most instructive discussion on what his gospel is and how he carries on his ministry.

II. Appeal to Complete the Collection (II Cor., chs. 8 and 9).

III. Vigorous Self-defense and Attack Upon the Selfish Intruders at Corinth (II Cor., chs. 10 to 13).

Passages to Read Again: Christian comfort (II Cor. 1: 3-7); living letters of recommendation (II Cor. 3: 1-3); the source of Paul's adequacy for his work (II Cor. 3: 4-6); the Christian worker's text (II Cor. 4: 5); the heart of the gospel (II Cor. 5: 17-21); the hardships Paul endured in the service of Christ (II Cor. 6: 4-10; 11: 23-29).

CHAPTER 13

The Letter to the Romans

PAUL kept moving on. His work was to preach in new places and found new churches (Rom. 15: 20). Born in Tarsus, educated in Jerusalem, converted near Damascus, he had finally become a leader at Antioch in Syria. From there he struck out in his missionary travels, and the direction of his work was westward. He did not move in a straight line, but he worked in Cyprus, southern and central Asia Minor, Macedonia, Greece, and finally in Ephesus.

His fruitful work at Ephesus, he thought, ended his pioneer work in the eastern part of the Roman Empire. Others were preaching in Palestine, Syria, and northern Asia Minor. Of first century churches in Egypt we know nothing, but the way Paul avoided it suggests that others were taking the gospel there. Where should he go next?

His mind turned to Spain. There an open field invited him. So he began to plan for a journey to Spain to preach in the Roman provinces there (Rom. 15: 24, 28). First he revisited Macedonia and Greece, especially to make sure that all was well at Corinth. Then he intended to take to Jerusalem the collection for the destitute Christians in Palestine (Rom. 15: 25-28). These things done, he could turn westward.

"I Must Also See Rome"

But to begin his work in the West he first had to go to Rome (Acts 19: 21). Two reasons drew him to that city. One was the church there; for years he had heard of it and planned to visit it, but so far he had been so busy in the East that he had never been able to do so (Rom. 1: 10, 13).

The other reason was the importance of Rome itself. Here was the capital city of the powerful Roman Empire. Here lived the rulers and leaders of the ancient world. To this center every province of the widespread Empire looked. From this city the famous Roman roads and well-traveled sea lanes led out in all directions. Paul himself was a Roman citizen, and he knew well the power and importance of Rome. He wanted to go there and preach.

Not that he wanted to settle down in Rome to live. Since there was already a church in the city, he would soon move on. But two things could come from the visit. One was the joy of preaching in so central and important a city. The other was the friendship of the Roman Christians. Only if they approved and supported him could he hope to do his work in Spain. If they suspected or opposed him they could make his work in the west difficult, and they might prevent any success. But if they were his friends and showed active interest in him, they would protect him against unfair attack and be of great help in all that he did.

Yet he did not know this church. He had never visited Italy. He did have a few friends there. Christians from churches he had founded or visited had gone to Rome. But the great majority of the Roman Christians had never seen him. They might even be prejudiced against him, for his enemies in other places might have sent to Rome unfair reports about him. So his first task was to win the friendship of the Roman Christians and thus prepare for his work in Spain. It was to show them his good will, invite their help, and explain how he understood the gospel that he wrote the letter to the Romans. He dictated and sent it about A.D. 57 or 58, during a three months' winter stay in Greece (Acts 20: 1-3), and probably while he was at Corinth.

How Was the Roman Church Founded?

Who founded the Roman Church? And when? Oddly enough, we cannot answer such questions. The Roman Catholic Church used to claim that the apostle Peter came to Rome about A.D. 42 and founded the Church, of which he was then the bishop and pope until his martyr death about A.D. 67. Today no Protestant or non-Christian scholar holds this view, and even some scholarly Roman Catholic books do not claim so much. One thing is certain: Peter was not the first to bring the gospel to Rome. He came there later; this is widely agreed, though it does not imply that he was pope. But he did not found the church there, and since Paul's letter does not refer to him, he was not at Rome when Paul wrote.

The gospel reached Rome in some other way. The earliest possible date was just after Pentecost. When God gave the Holy Spirit to the waiting disciples, people from Rome, we are told, were present (Acts 2: 10). Some of these Roman pilgrims may have been converted, and if so, they took the gospel to Rome. Or perhaps Christians whom Paul or some other leader had converted in the East went to Rome, told the gospel story, and founded the church.

Only two things are certain. This church was established early, and when Paul wrote, it had a wide reputation as a strong church (Rom. 1: 8). It is easy to understand why Paul wanted to visit it, and how it could help or hinder his work in Spain.

Paul's earlier letters went to churches he had founded and guided. In them he frequently refers to past events and to his personal actions. Since he and the churches addressed knew each other personally, the letters could be informal and they dealt with specific situations. But in writing to Rome, Paul addresses a group almost all of whom are strangers to him. The letter reflects this. It is more formal and less personal.

To be sure, Paul knew some facts about the situation at

Rome. He knew that most of the Christians there were Gentiles (Rom. 1: 13; 11: 13) but that there were also enough Jewish Christians to make the relation of Christianity to Judaism a live issue. He knew too that the Christians had to decide whether to obey the pagan Empire (Rom. 13: 1-7), and that they were disputing as to whether they should eat certain foods (Rom. 14: 1 to 15: 13). But even so, the letter lacks the personal touch of his letters to churches he knew.

The Gospel that God Alone Can Save

What does Paul have to say to this strong and important church? Does he know some striking new truth to interest and surprise them? Not at all. He has no new story to tell. Paul and the Roman church both have the same gospel, and he presents the heart of that gospel to the Romans, to help them and to win their friendship. It is the gospel for Jews and Gentiles alike, for the Empire and indeed for the world, for faith and for daily life, for the present and for the future.

Paul did not invent it. He received it (Gal. 1: 11, 12). It is "the gospel of God" (Rom. 1: 1), the story of what God has done for men through Christ. It is the gospel that God can and will save all men who believe in the good news that he offers salvation in Christ.

To tell where he stands and why he writes, Paul recalls that the gospel had its origin in Israel; that Jesus Christ was of Davidic descent but is also the Son of God with power; that, through Christ, God offers salvation to all men; and that God has sent Paul to preach especially to Gentiles (Rom. 1: 1-7). Paul then thanks God for the good reports about the Roman church's faith. He assures them that he has long prayed and is still praying that he may visit them and preach in Rome (Rom. 1: 8-15).

Now Paul states his great theme. Even in Rome, the proud and mighty capital of the Empire, he will not be ashamed of the gospel. Rome may have great military and political power, but the real power, the power to save men, God gives in the gospel. The right relation to God and the right life are open to all who believe (Rom. 1: 16,17).

No doubt there were persons then as today who felt no need to be saved. Paul knew they were wrong. Every man fails; before God he stands as a sinner. So Paul first describes the sin and need of all men, Jew and Gentile alike (Rom. 1: 18 to 3: 20). By observing men and studying Scripture he knew well their evil and failure. Even the Jews, who had had great advantages, were as guilty of sin as the Gentiles. Not even the law and instruction in the Scriptures had prevented this. Men, all men, share a common need. They deserve God's judgment; they need help that they themselves cannot find.

That help came in Christ, who at great cost provided redemption for all who believe. Since God sent Christ and so saved man, no man can proudly give the credit to himself or to his own group. His new position and privilege is God's undeserved gift, freely offered to all men. Though at first it was offered to the Jews, now in God's plan all peoples can receive it on the one basis of sincere faith (Rom. 3: 21-31).

By this way of salvation God's free grace saves sinful, helpless men. This was not the way the law worked. Under it a man earns or loses his standing by keeping or breaking the law. Yet the gospel of free salvation through faith in Christ has deep roots in the Old Testament and the life of Israel (Rom., ch. 4). In fact, two of the most honored Jewish forefathers illustrate truths of the gospel. It was really Abraham's faith that God approved in him (Gen. 15: 6), and David in Ps. 32 spoke of forgiveness as the way to fellowship with God. God's forgiving grace and man's answering faith are basic parts of the gospel.

This faith not only opens the way to God; it leads on to a life of strong character. It assures the believer, for whom Christ died, that God will give still greater blessings through his Spirit. God's saving power will prove complete victor over the devastating effects of man's sin. And the ground of this confidence is never in man's greatness; it is always in God, who meets man's need in the crucified and living Christ. The Jewish law had only a secondary role; it made clear what man should do but did not do, and so it brought out the fact that man in his sin must turn to Christ for help (Rom., ch. 5).

The Christian Breaks with Sin

To those of evil impulses this gospel may seem an invitation to sin as much as possible. If God forgives freely, if man's great sin only makes God's goodness stand out more clearly, why not go on sinning? Why not sin more, so that God will get more credit for saving such wicked men?

To Paul such an attitude was unthinkable. What does it mean to believe in Christ and accept the gift God gives through him? It means much more than to say that the gospel is true. Of course faith includes belief, but it is more than mere belief. It means to put personal trust in Christ. It means to give one's life to God in grateful loyalty. True faith links the life to God, so that the Christian can never think that God's grace leaves him free to be as evil as he likes.

Since Paul knew that this problem bothered many people, he deals with it at length (Rom. 6: 1 to 8: 39). To believe sincerely, to dedicate one's life to Christ, means a break with the sinful past. To use Paul's picture, it means to die to sin and rise, as Christ did, to a new life. He who accepts in faith the grace God offers must turn from his wrong ways, break with evil ties that drag him down, and then live life with a new center in Christ and a new power in the Holy Spirit.

The center and control of life is no longer man's selfish, sinful purpose. Nor is it the external law. It is rather Christ, man's Lord and Redeemer. The law was good (Rom. 7: 12). It prescribed good acts. But it did not give men the power to break the grip of evil on their life. It demanded much, but did not give the power to do it. So it led to a cry of despair (Rom.

7: 24), to which Christ brings the answer. In the life of the loyal believer the Holy Spirit gives power to be faithful and confident (Rom., ch. 8).

Thus the love of God, already shown in Christ, now leads man through the Spirit to a life of grateful obedience. Trusting in God's steadfast purpose, the Christian faces the future with hope and lives in the spirit of victory. He still must struggle, and sometimes he may falter, but the gospel has given him power. With Paul he can say, "For I am sure that neither death, nor life, nor angels, nor principalities, nor things present, nor things to come, nor powers, nor height, nor depth, nor anything else in all creation, will be able to separate us from the love of God in Christ Jesus our Lord" (Rom. 8: 38, 39).

The Jews and Christ

This is the gospel for all men. But why, Paul asks with a sad heart, have not more Jews believed? The gospel has spread and won numerous Gentiles. But the Jewish leaders and the majority of the Jews have rejected Christ and many have even fought the Christians. This tragedy gives Paul, a Jew deeply grateful for his Jewish heritage, unceasing agony of spirit. The gospel came "to the Jew first" (Rom. 1: 16), and yet most Jews reject it. How can Christians explain this? How are Christian Jews to think of it? What attitude should Gentile Christians take toward the Jews? These questions must have troubled the Roman church as well as Paul, so in Rom., chs. 9 to 11, he discusses them for this mainly Gentile church.

With heavy heart Paul recalls how the Jews have failed to use rightly their God-given privileges (Rom. 9: 1-5). Then he comes to his main point. God is always the sovereign Lord of the world. If in his power and wisdom he chooses to build a mainly Gentile church and leave most members of Judaism outside, man cannot condemn him. He has the right to choose among men and work out his will by the workers whom he selects (Rom. 9: 6-33).

This does not mean that God acts without wisdom or justice. Paul knows that God is just, even when men cannot understand his ways. And in this case there is more to say. The Jews have heard the gospel. They are guilty of rejecting Christ (Rom., ch. 10). Yet even so, not all Jews have refused the gospel. A remnant, a part, have believed, just as in past times at least some of God's people have always been faithful (Rom. 11: 1-10).

But even so God has brought good out of sinful unbelief. The Jews have rejected the gospel, persecuted the Christians, and driven them out into the Gentile world. With what result? The gospel has been preached to more people than ever before, and multitudes of Gentiles have believed. So a benefit has come from the tragic refusal of Jews to believe (Rom. 11: 11-24). Besides, Paul expects that in the end, after the gospel has reached all nations, the Jews will yet believe and so God will "have mercy upon all" (Rom. 11: 25-32).

Paul does not understand all the ways of God. But he trusts God; he believes that God in superior wisdom is working out his just and kindly will among men. So his last word on this theme is one of trust and praise (Rom. 11: 33-36).

Guidance for Christian Living

The Christian can walk in "newness of life" (Rom. 6: 4). So to the Roman church, as to other churches, Paul points out what the gospel demands in daily living. They must present their bodies a living sacrifice, pure and dedicated to God. They must be so changed that now all their thinking and action serve God's purpose. So in every way they will gladly show Christian love and helpfulness (Rom., ch. 12). Even when faced with active evil, they will act with good will: "Do not be overcome by evil, but overcome evil with good" (Rom. 12: 21).

In the Empire this requires Christians to obey the law and perform their duty (Rom. 13: 1-7). In all relations, it demands that they live with love for every neighbor (Rom. 13: 8-10). Life is urgent; the end is too near to waste time and risk ruin by low living (Rom. 13: 11-14).

Some Christians had scruples against eating meats. Perhaps they feared that they might eat meat that had been sacrificed to idols, and so seem to approve idolatry (cf. I Cor., chs. 8; 10). Other Christians held, and Paul personally agreed with them, that a Christian could eat any wholesome meat and thank God for it. But no Christian can scorn a weaker Christian's conscience, nor should those who have scruples accuse a stronger brother's conscience of treason to Christ. In things that are not essential each side should respect the judgment of others; each person should take care not to hurt the conscience of his fellow Christian (Rom. 14: 1 to 15: 13).

So ends the main part of the letter. Paul then explains his plans (Rom. 15: 14-33). He has finished his work in the East. After taking the collection to Jerusalem, he intends to visit Rome on his way to Spain. He knows there is danger in Jerusalem. (Indeed, there within a few months he was mobbed, arrested, and sent to Rome as a prisoner.) But he never let fear of danger guide his life.

A Separate Letter to Ephesus?

The letter seems finished. But another chapter follows. Although Paul wrote the Epistle to the Romans to a church he never had visited, ch. 16 gives personal greetings to dozens of Christians. Paul even knows that certain ones gather in little groups and he knows also in whose houses the groups meet. Did all these personal friends live in Rome? Shortly before Paul wrote this letter, Aquila and Priscilla were in Ephesus (Acts 18: 19; I Cor. 16: 19). Later, according to II Tim. 4: 19, they were not at Rome and probably were at Ephesus. Did they move back from Ephesus to Rome for a time, gather a church together in their house (Rom. 16: 3), and then return again to Ephesus before the time of Second Timothy? Again, Paul calls Epaenetus the "first fruits" of Asia (Rom. 16: 5), that is, the first convert made in western Asia, where Ephesus was located. Had he moved to Rome? Or should we look for these friends of Paul in Ephesus?

Is it possible that Paul wrote Rom., ch. 16, or at least Rom. 16: 1-20, as a note to Ephesus, and that it later was attached to his letter to Rome? Certainly at Ephesus, where Paul worked for three years, he would know many Christians and their home situations. We know from ancient manuscripts and writers that some copies of Romans lacked the last chapter, or even the last two chapters. On the other hand, we may suppose that many of Paul's friends had moved to Rome and kept in touch with him, and that here, to make the most of every personal tie with the church at Rome, he closes the letter by mentioning his friends by name.

Why Do We Still Read the Epistle to the Romans?

Paul's letter to Rome is not the easiest book in the world to read. It is not a story; it deals with difficult topics; it calls for the reader's earnest attention. Why should the Christian read and reread it? For at least three reasons:

First of all, it is perhaps the greatest work Paul ever wrote. Certainly nowhere else does he state so carefully the gospel he preaches. He is not driven by crisis to rapid and indignant attack, as he is in Galatians. He takes up few purely local problems such as most of his letters discuss. Here he presents his faith quietly and in its full strength, so that the Romans can see what he believes and why he preaches so untiringly.

Then, too, this letter has proved one of the most powerful books the Church has ever known. Again and again a fresh study of Romans has given new light and vigor when the Church was confused or wavering. At the Reformation, for example, Romans did much to give to Luther and Calvin and others the message and urgency that made them strong.

Finally, in this letter we still can find the deep truths of our faith. God gives the gospel. It comes as his free gift to sinful men. He asks only sincere faith that gives the whole life to him in response. This gospel is no idle idea; it contains the power of God to change men's lives. It brings the active power of goodness into everyday human life. It is for all men of all nations. "It is the power of God for salvation to every one who has faith" (Rom. 1: 16).

The world needs this message. Our Church needs to hear it so that we may always remember where our help is found. But this letter reminds Christians that this gospel is not only God's gift to them but also a call to world-wide mission work. A strong Church will thank God for Romans, read it, and live by what it teaches.

READING HINTS: Nothing takes the place of reading the entire letter. But the following passages deserve special attention: Paul's debt to all men (Rom. 1: 14, 15); the theme of the letter (Rom. 1: 16, 17); God's gift of righteousness through faith (Rom. 3: 21-26); God gives power for good living through Christ (Rom., ch. 6); the Spirit-led life and its promise of eternal blessings (Rom., ch. 8); the Christian's daily life (Rom., ch. 12); love fulfills the law (Rom. 13: 8-10).

CHAPTER 14

Philemon and Colossians

THERE WERE CHURCHES in cities Paul never saw that owed their beginning to him. One of these was at Colossae, a city a hundred miles east of Ephesus. While Paul was in Ephesus, people from Colossae and other cities of that region kept coming to Ephesus, and some heard him preach. In fact, Luke tells us in a sweeping statement that "all the residents of Asia heard the word of the Lord, both Jews and Greeks" (Acts 19: 10). Demetrius the silversmith, in rousing the Ephesian mob against Paul, asserts that "almost throughout all Asia this Paul has persuaded and turned away a considerable company of people" (Acts 19: 26). Travelers came to Ephesus for business, sightseeing, or pleasure. The great temple of Artemis drew multitudes of worshipers, especially at the time of the great yearly festival. Some of these visitors heard Paul, and those who believed in Christ took the gospel story home with them.

Nor was this the only way Paul used to spread the gospel. He sent out his helpers into surrounding cities to preach to people he never could see. It may be that he sent Epaphras to Colossae to preach and unite the first Christians there into a church (Col. 1: 7; 4: 12; Philemon 23).

PHILEMON THE CHRISTIAN

One well-to-do man of Colossae who met and heard Paul in Ephesus was Philemon. Paul speaks to him in words of warm personal friendship, and reminds him that he owes to Paul his very life (Philemon 19). This does not mean that Paul had saved him from physical danger, but that through Paul the gospel, which gives true life, had come to Philemon. Since Paul says that he had never been in Colossae (Col. 2: 1), Philemon must have met him elsewhere, and this happened most likely in Ephesus.

From the time of conversion Philemon had been an earnest, active Christian. He had been eager to give friendly help to other Christians. His home had become a center of Christian worship and influence (Philemon 2, 5). The local church had no building, and Philemon's hospitality made possible common meals and meetings for worship that bound the church together. Thus he led the church in its earliest and neediest years.

Letters from Prison

With such new churches Paul kept in close touch. No doubt he sent to them messengers and letters of which we have no word. But we know that two letters went to Colossae to help them in special problems they had to meet.

These problems arose at a time when we might excuse Paul for doing nothing. He was in prison (Philemon 1, 9; Col. 4: 10, 18). But where? As he told the Corinthians (II Cor. 11: 23), he had endured "far more imprisonments" than his critics had. One was at Philippi (Acts 16: 23). But he was not in prison there long enough to receive visitors and write letters. If we were to take I Cor. 15: 32 literally, we might suggest that Paul was once in prison at Ephesus, and while there wrote one or more of his prison letters (Philemon, Colossians, Ephesians, and Philippians). Most likely, however, he wrote these letters during the imprisonment reported in the closing chapters of The Acts. He wrote probably not during the two years at Caesarea (Acts 24: 27), but about A.D. 61 or 62, during the two years at Rome (Acts 28: 30). News reached him there that led him to write Philemon and Colossians.

Onesimus the Slave

The letter to Philemon concerned a slave of Philemon, Onesimus, who evidently had seized some of his master's property and fled to Rome (Philemon 18). How he got in touch with Paul at Rome we are not told. He may have been with Philemon in Ephesus and met Paul there, so that when he needed a friend in Rome, he thought of Paul and knew how to find him. Possibly he had heard of Paul in Philemon's home at Colossae, and knew that Paul was a friend of slaves. Perhaps Epaphras, who had been in Colossae and was then in Rome with Paul, met Onesimus and led him to talk to Paul. The important thing is that he did meet Paul and was led by Paul to put his faith in Christ (Philemon 10).

But what should the slave do, now that he had become a Christian? Paul told him that he should return to his master, whom he had wronged, and prove himself worthy of trust. He should go back where he had failed and start there. Onesimus was willing to go. So Paul sent him back.

This was a dangerous step. The owner of a criminal slave could beat, imprison, or even put to death his dishonest servant. Paul cared too much for Onesimus to send him into such danger without giving him all the help he could. In three ways he acted to protect the returning slave. He no doubt instructed Tychicus, who carried the letters to Colossae, to speak personally on behalf of Onesimus. Then, too, in his letter to the entire Colossian church he recommended Onesimus as "the faithful and beloved brother, who is one of yourselves" (Col. 4: 9). He also wrote directly to Philemon and his household to intercede for the repentant wrongdoer.

The Letter to Philemon

The letter to Philemon is not a private note. Paul addresses not only Philemon, but also his wife Apphia, and Archippus, probably his son, and in addition the group of Christians who met for worship in that home. He thus puts Philemon "on the spot." The entire group will hear the letter and will watch to see whether Philemon shows the Christian spirit of forgiveness in dealing with his slave.

To strengthen the appeal and to give Philemon his due, Paul thanks God for all the good deeds his friend has done (Philemon 4-7). He then asks as a favor that Philemon forgive and welcome back his now Christian slave. Paul does not dictate the decision, but he appeals with every art he knows (Philemon 8-22). He makes an interesting play on the Greek word *onēsimos,* which means "profitable." Paul admits that the slave was once untrue to his name, but points out that now he has become profitable, and warns Philemon to be sure that his own life now proves profitable to his Lord (Philemon 11, 20).

Continuing the bookkeeping idea, Paul offers to assume the debt that Onesimus owes Philemon for the things he stole (Philemon 18). Paul could never pay the debt, and does not expect Philemon to ask him to do so, but the offer permits him to add that he had been the one to convert Philemon, so that if they balanced accounts Philemon would still be in debt to Paul. What he really wants, then, is for Philemon to receive back his slave and forgive the debt. To put still more pressure on Philemon, Paul reports that he hopes to be released soon and visit Colossae (Philemon 22). This warns Philemon to treat Onesimus in such a Christian way that he will not be ashamed to face Paul when he comes.

Paul had wanted to keep Onesimus with him. He needed friends to care for him in prison and help him in the work he still was doing for Christ. But he felt he must send the slave back home. Yet he hints that he expects Philemon to "do even more than I say" (Philemon 21). Does he mean that he wants Philemon to set the slave free? Some have thought so. But this is not certain. Two other explanations are possible. Since he has offered to assume the debt Onesimus owes, Paul may be hinting that he expects Philemon freely to forgive that debt. Or, since he has said that he would like to have Onesimus with him (Philemon 13), he may be suggesting that he expects Philemon to send the slave back to help him. The fact that Philemon kept the letter surely indicates that Paul at least won for Onesimus the full forgiveness he asked.

The Gospel and Slavery

Nowhere in this letter does Paul flatly condemn slavery. Indeed, when, in Col. 3: 18 to 4: 1, he speaks of the various members of the household, he carefully tells the slaves to be obedient and not rebellious. He did not fight to abolish slavery. In the autocratic Empire, where he had no political voice or vote, and where Christians were but a handful of the population, he could do nothing directly to change the system.

This troubles many people. They feel that the Christians in their homes could have broken with the system. No doubt many did. But certain facts will help us to understand Paul better. He did not expect the world to last for centuries; his primary concern was to convert as many as possible with the greatest possible speed. Moreover, he wanted to put the emphasis in the right place. The basic thing was faith in Christ and mutual friendship among Christians. He brought people of all classes into one fellowship, so that the slave became "a beloved brother" (Philemon 16). It would be wrong for us to stop where Paul did, now that we have great numbers and active citizenship, but it still is true that personal faith and voluntary helpfulness are more vital than laws and external organization.

Another fact is important. By faith and Christian living Onesimus became worthy of respect and freedom. In ancient Greek a slave was sometimes called a "body." He was not regarded as a person; he was just a working machine. But in Christian faith slaves became true persons, and Paul and other Christians treated them as brothers. In the long run, that doomed slavery. It could not endure when the slave became a real person and a Christian brother.

An Attempt to Combine Religions

Is Christianity just one religion among many good ones? Are they all to be combined? At Colossae, where Philemon lived, Christians were confused about this. All around them in Asia Minor, all sorts of religions existed. Greek idolatry, nature religions which worshiped the heavenly bodies and the powers of nature, superstitious magical rites, asceticism which tortured the body to try to help the soul, mystery religions which promised by secret ceremonies to redeem man now and for the life to come—all these met and combined. Polytheism, the worship of many gods, was so often taken for granted that people saw no wrong in combining several such religions. Even when they decided that there was only one God, they saw no difference between the God of the Christians and the fickle or immoral gods of other religions.

The Christians of Colossae lived in this lenient atmosphere. They found people willing to listen to their gospel, but the hearers were not so clear as Paul was that "although there may be so-called gods . . . yet for us there is one God, the Father, from whom are all things and for whom we exist, and one Lord, Jesus Christ, through whom are all things and through whom we exist" (I Cor. 8: 5, 6). Some who shared in pagan religions and philosophies had also adopted some Jewish practices, and now were ready to pay reverence also to Jesus and accept parts of the Christian teaching. This they thought wise, broad-minded, and tolerant. Evidently some in the church at Colossae were tempted by this attitude. They were inclined to regard Jesus as only one of a number of divine lords to whom they could look for help.

Indeed, they tended to put Jesus below some of the other divine beings they worshiped. Perhaps they shared the widespread ancient view that physical matter is inherently evil, so that to live a physical life means to live on a lower level than do pure spiritual beings such as angels. Jesus might help men. He was a messenger from God. But since he lived in a physical body he was not so pure and perfect as the angels, and so could not give such help as they could or deserve so much reverence as they did. Such ideas gave Jesus an inferior rank below the angels; it made normal physical life seem evil; it encouraged Christians to avoid marriage and to torture the body by strict ascetic rules to suppress all physical pleasure.

To judge by the tone of confidence with which Paul writes, the Colossian Christians had not adopted such ideas, except in rare cases. He believes that most of them are fully loyal to Christ (Col. 1: 3-12). But this new church needs wise guidance. Perhaps Epaphras has urged him to write and state the Christian truth for the help of these new and confused Christians.

Christ Fully Meets Man's Needs

Paul's central theme is clear. Jesus Christ is the one and sufficient Saviour of men. He rightly claims the full faith and loyalty of them all. There is no need and no place for all the angel worship, legalistic rules, and ascetic practices by which some Colossians were tempted to think they could reach God. In Jesus Christ, God has come to them; the Son has made the Father known, and given redemption and new life to all believers. He is the one Head of the Church. There is room for no rival. So before Paul condemns the false ideas that some are urging the Colossians to accept, he states his full faith in Christ, in words that leave no room for such wrong views (Col. 1: 13-23).

It is a tremendous faith. It covers the full sweep of history and all that God does. The Son is the Father's image; he is the divine agent in creating all things; he upholds all and carries out the divine will in history; he entered into history in order to redeem men and become the Head of the Church, of which he is the risen Lord. All creation must look to him as its Head.

Even the angels are his creation and owe to him their redemption. Plainly, then, they are not his superiors or equals, nor are they worthy of worship. Worship belongs to God alone, and the Son as divine shares in that worship, which all created beings should offer.

The Church therefore must look to Christ alone for the answer to its needs. And it will never look in vain if it looks in faith. To be sure, men like Paul serve Christ as ministers, and even suffer in their work (Col. 1: 24-29). But their message is not that they are great men; they too are sinners, and owe their salvation to Christ. They speak rather of "Christ in you, the hope of glory" (Col. 1: 27). The believer, linked by faith with the living Christ, receives from him resources sufficient to meet every test now and in the future, and may look forward with sturdy hope to a final happiness even greater than his present blessings.

Since this is so, Christians should live in ever-deepening faith and loyalty to Christ (Col. 2: 1-7). In Christ, God is fully present; they are not to think that only a fragment of God is in him, so that they must seek the rest in the angels and worship them. They are not to think that by ascetic practices and special rules they can lift themselves and earn their way to God (Col. 2: 8-23). Forgiveness and new life is God's gift. It is futile and wicked to lose sight of this fact in a vain and busy effort to rebuild one's own marred life. That only confuses the truth about the greatness of Christ, and stirs up sinful pride in man. The Christian is to live gratefully on the high level of the new life that the risen Christ gives him (Col. 3: 1-4).

Every evil act and thought must be completely given up. Instead, the disciple is to follow with willing, complete, loving reverence the example and will of Christ (Col. 3: 5-17). "Whatever you do, in word or deed, do everything in the name of the Lord Jesus, giving thanks to God the Father through him." (Col. 3: 17.)

Christian love and unselfishness are to govern each member

of the household. Some think, with reason, that under our changed social conditions the place Paul gave to women must be redefined. But he had firm hold of the essential point for all: each member of the family is to think, not of rights, but of the privilege of showing active love and helpfulness (Col. 3: 18 to 4: 1).

The Wider Ties of Christian Faith

Again and again, as in Col. 4: 2-18, the closing part of Paul's letters reminds the Christians addressed that in many places they have Christian friends, with whom they are bound together in prayer and friendship. They must live winsomely with all other men (Col. 4: 5, 6), but their bond with Christians is the deepest one.

This letter mentions a special way in which the Colossians will get a wider view. In nearby Laodicea there is also a church. A letter is going to that church. Paul wants it read in Colossae also. He further wants the letter to the Colossians to be read in Laodicea. Paul is pointing the churches beyond their own local communities, and giving them a sense of the one great Church in which Christ unites all believers. Then, too, the exchange of Paul's letters started the process that led in time to a full collection of these letters and to the formation of the New Testament.

Reading Hints: After you have read the letter to Philemon, make a list of the many ways in which Paul appeals to Philemon or puts pressure on him to forgive Onesimus.

As you read Colossians, note: Paul's interest in Christians he never saw (Col. 1: 3-12); the work of the Son (Col. 1: 13-23); Paul's work and suffering to bring Christ to the Gentiles (Col. 1: 24 to 2: 3); the new life with Christ (Col. 3: 1-4); the picture of daily Christian living (Col. 3: 12-17).

CHAPTER 15

The Letter Called "Ephesians"

"BEHOLD, how good and how pleasant it is for brethren to dwell together in unity!"

These words of Ps. 133: 1 express how Paul thought of the Church. The Church of Christ should be united. He constantly prayed that it might live in Christian harmony. Since "the Church's one Foundation is Jesus Christ her Lord," since there is but one gospel (Gal. 1: 7), there can be but one Church, and all who believe in Christ are members of one great brotherhood.

Paul held to his deep concern for the unity of the Church in spite of discouraging tendencies to division. Did not the church at Corinth split into parties (I Cor. 1: 12)? Yes, unfortunately it did. Was it not a constant struggle to get Jewish and Gentile Christians to understand each other and live together in peace? Indeed it was. Why then did he not act as we modern Christians do and organize a number of denominations, so that each party or group could have its own organization and officers and its own separate place of meeting? That seems so simple a solution. But for Paul it was impossible. To the Corinthians he at once retorted, "Is Christ divided?" (I Cor. 1:13). All followers of the one Christ belong together in one Church. To those who made it hard for Jewish and Gentile Christians to live together he declared, "There is neither Jew nor Greek, . . . for you are all one in Christ Jesus" (Gal. 3: 28). To divide the Church along lines of race or class or any other grouping is thus entirely wrong.

We come now to the letter that more than any other writing of Paul lays emphasis on this theme of Christian unity. As you read Eph. 4: 1-6, you will note how he hammers home this vital truth. All through the letter the same truth stands out. The key words that Paul uses show where he centers his interest. Eighteen times we find "one," "unite," or "unity." The words "all" and "every" occur over forty times in all. Paul is determined to express as clearly as he can that this is the one gospel for the one world Church.

Unity Through Faith in Christ

The letter has two main divisions. In the first half (Eph., chs. 1 to 3) Paul describes the unity of the Church. It has its one head in Christ, and it unites all its members in one fellowship of faith and worship. This unity goes back to the one God, who gives life and direction to all the generations of men. Through all history his one divine plan is at work. That plan has its center in Christ, in whom God has summed up the whole divine purpose, and it is carried forward by the Holy Spirit, given to those who believe in Christ (Eph. 1: 3-14). So Paul prays that his readers may all grow in understanding of the full meaning of the gospel, and that they may appreciate more fully that Christ is the Lord of all God's creatures (Eph. 1: 15-23).

All mankind once shared a most unhappy lot. All men were in the grip of sin and so were without real life. Then came the rescue from this sin and the finding of new life. There is only one way to this blessing, the freely given grace of God in Christ (Eph. 2: 1-10). It is what God does that saves man. Man may keep trying to save some of the credit for himself; he may say that at least his faith is to his credit. Paul warns against all such pride in man's doing; in every step to new life it is God at work. Even the faith by which man accepts what God does for him is prompted by God; Paul says that it is "the gift of God" (Eph. 2: 8).

This one gospel unites all men. Formerly the Jews and Gentiles seemed sharply separated. God had indeed given the Jews many gifts, but when it came to finding the way to God and good living, Jews and Gentiles found themselves in the same need. They both were saved in the same way, by the death and seeking ministry of the now risen Christ. The old dividing wall has been broken down. All men now join in the one great Church of which Christ is the chief cornerstone. All form one great growing temple of God (Eph. 2: 11-22).

In this world Church Paul's task is to take the gospel to the Gentiles. God has sent him to tell the Gentiles that they are now full partners with the Jews in the one universal Church (Eph. 3: 1-13). This is a message rich in its meaning for Christian worship and living. Paul earnestly prays that God will help the readers to understand this gospel more and more fully, and he praises God for the many blessings he graciously gives to those who gratefully worship him (Eph. 3: 14-21).

Unity in Christian Living

What does this confident faith mean for life? If the one God provides the one way of salvation through the one Saviour and Lord Jesus Christ, if this gift is open to all on the one basis of faith, if all are thus united in the one world Church, then this must lead to unity in daily Christian living (Eph., chs. 4 to 6).

Through the work of the one Lord Christ and by the leading power of the one Holy Spirit, God brings men together and enables them to live together. He does not do this by making them all alike. He uses many leaders, but to no two of them does he give the same gifts. He calls each one to use his special abilities to serve the needs of the one Church. In God's plan this varied leadership unites the Church in common worship and mutual good will. The grateful Christians all work together for each other's good (Eph. 4: 1-16).

The Christians of Paul's day knew well the pagan world. Not only were the great majority of their neighbors pagans, but they themselves had come into the Christian life from a pagan background. In their younger years they had not known a Christian home. So there was always danger that pagan ways of thinking and living would continue to influence them. Therefore Paul keeps urging them to put away their former way of life and act as new men. In daily life they are to shun all coarse and impure living; they must live honestly and with love, and be ever alert and thankful (Eph. 4: 17 to 5: 20).

In this letter as in Colossians, Paul urges the members of the home to show mutual respect and love (Eph. 5: 21 to 6: 9). But here a new thought appears. As Paul thinks of the love of husband and wife, he sees in it a symbol of the faithful love between Christ and the Church. For the Church exists only in close unity with Christ and in loyal service to him. But this thought does not make Paul forget the home. Its unity depends upon mutual love, helpfulness, and respect. Each member of the family circle, in all that he does, is to do the will of God; the life that does God's will is a life of love and willing care for others' welfare.

In an earlier letter Paul had spoken of the soldier's equipment, to teach how the Christian must serve his commander or Lord (I Thess. 5: 8). Now he uses this illustration again, and quite naturally, for he is a prisoner and under the constant watch of armed soldiers. He uses it to show how the Christian must protect himself against all attacks on his faith, and battle skillfully for the cause he serves (Eph. 6: 10-20). He twice urges that one must use the whole armor God supplies, just as a soldier does not feel protected or equipped unless he has put on all the parts of the armor that his leader gives him. Back of this appeal is Paul's clear knowledge that life is a struggle between good and evil forces. Each person must enlist under the right commander and serve in a steadfast, active way.

In the closing words Paul sends news and offers a final prayer for the readers (Eph. 6: 21-24). Victory in life's battle depends on the constant gifts of God and on the Christian's faithful response of grateful love.

A General Letter to Many Churches

To whom did Paul write this letter? Amazing as it may seem, Ephesians was not written only to Ephesus. To be sure, in earlier English translations of the Bible Eph. 1: 1 contains the words "in Ephesus." But the Revised Standard Version and other modern translations rightly omit these words. They occur in the late Greek manuscripts of the letter, but the earliest and best manuscripts do not have them. This shows that they were not in the original copy. Paul did not address this letter to Ephesus, but "to the saints who are also faithful in Christ Jesus."

The very nature of the letter supports this conclusion. Paul had worked in Ephesus for nearly three years. How could he write a letter to so well-known a church without making personal references to his friends there or to his work in that city? In his other letters he speaks to his churches in words of warm friendship; personal references and memories continually appear. But here in Ephesians the tone is general; what he says lacks local color. In fact, he never says to the readers that he has preached to them. He only tells them that he has heard of their faith and assumes that they have heard of his ministry (Eph. 1: 15; 3: 2).

Thus Ephesians is different from all the other letters of Paul we have studied. Even the letters to Rome and Colossae, places he never had visited, contain more specific and direct references to his work and his readers. How can we explain this general tone of Ephesians?

One answer has been that Paul wrote this letter to a church that he knew of but never had visited. Perhaps, it has been suggested, he wrote it to Laodicea, near Colossae. This, then, may be "the letter from Laodicea" of which Col. 4: 16 speaks. As early as the second century, Marcion and others seem to have called it "Laodiceans" instead of "Ephesians." But a serious difficulty arises; this letter is so general that it does not describe or reflect the situation in a single local church. If we compare Ephesians with Colossians, which was written to a church Paul never had visited, it is clear at once that Colossians has far more definite reference to local conditions.

So Ephesians must have gone to more than one church. To some scholars it seems so general that they doubt whether Paul wrote it at all. They suppose that some follower of Paul wrote this general epistle, to sum up Paul's teaching and assist in making Paul's other letters known. But the language is Paul's; the letter was known as Paul's from very early times.

The most likely view, therefore, is that when Paul wrote Philemon and Colossians, about A.D. 61 or 62, he also wrote this general letter. The same messenger, Tychicus (Col. 4: 7; Eph. 6: 21), was to carry all three letters, and was to read Ephesians to various churches in western Asia Minor. Because Paul sent it to be read to several churches, he omitted all local color. Because it was circulated in the region near Ephesus, a copy no doubt was made for the church there. That would help to explain why later copies of the letter inserted the words "in Ephesus." Christians knew that the letter had some connection with Ephesus.

Paul's situation in this letter is the same as in Philemon and Colossians. He is in prison (Philemon 1, 9, 10; Col. 4: 18; Eph. 3: 1; 4: 1). The letter carrier, Tychicus, delivered all three letters (Col. 4: 7; Eph. 6: 21). The language of Ephesians repeatedly parallels that of Colossians. Often, in writing two letters at one sitting, we use much of the same language in both. This, it seems, is what Paul did. After writing Philemon and Colossians to meet specific problems, he writes a more general letter to encourage and instruct other churches in the same region. For convenience, we may continue to call it Ephesians.

God's Plan to Unite All Things in Christ

The very fact that Paul here writes with no reference to local controversies and problems makes the letter more instructive to us. He writes without haste or argument. In a calm spirit and on a wide canvas he paints the broad picture of the gospel for the world. Here is his deep missionary faith. Here is the message for which he is ready to suffer and die.

Back of all Paul's mission work is his steady faith in God as the One to whom the gospel and every good gift are due. We understand history only when we see that in it God, through his chosen agents, is working out his purpose for men. This plan centers in Christ. It becomes effective in men as the Spirit of God leads them to believe in Christ and do his will. Each generation and each individual has a part to play. This plan includes Jew and Gentile alike. Thus there results one great world Church, so that no Christian can rest content as long as the Church is divided or has not spread into the entire world.

The right response to all these gifts of God is a life full of faith, gratitude, and joy. So in Paul the spirit of prayer finds repeated expression. He thanks God for the gospel (Eph. 1: 3-14), and for the Christian faith and lives of his readers (Eph. 1: 15-23). The prayer in Eph. 3: 1, broken off but resumed in Eph. 3: 14, is that they may ever grow in understanding and in loyal life. For such gifts he and they may pray with confidence; God's readiness to give is greater than man's readiness to ask or receive (Eph. 3: 14-21).

In the unity of the Christian brotherhood there is a place and need for every God-given talent. It is God's will that the Christian should grow; turning his back on every unworthy thing in his past life, he should grow in good will and in faithfulness to God. In every relationship and under every trial that evil and hardship bring, it is every believer's God-given mission to show this good will, loyalty, and helpfulness. Just as Paul desires, and asks the readers to pray, that he may have strength and courage to preach boldly, even though he is in chains (Eph. 6: 18-20), so every Christian is to find unity in his own life by undivided faith and unswerving doing of all that God gives him to do.

"I therefore . . . beg you . . . to maintain the unity of the Spirit in the bond of peace." "Be strong in the Lord and in the strength of his might." "Understand what the will of the Lord is." "Put on the new nature, created after the likeness of God in true righteousness and holiness." "Be kind to one another, tenderhearted, forgiving one another, as God in Christ forgave you." "Walk in love, as Christ loved us and gave himself up for us." "Always and for everything giving thanks in the name of our Lord Jesus Christ to God the Father."

READING HINTS: As you read, note the passages that speak of the one God, the one gospel, the unity of the Church, and the unity of all men in Christ. Watch for the words "one," "unite," "unity," "all," "every," and "each."

What are the things Paul says Christ does for us? What are the blessings the Spirit gives?

Passages for Special Study: "By grace you have been saved through faith" (Eph. 2: 1-10); Jew and Gentile united in Christ (Eph. 2: 11-22); Paul's prayer for his readers (Eph. 3: 14-19); "The unity of the Spirit" (Eph. 4: 1-16); "Walk in love" (Eph. 4: 25 to 6: 20); "The whole armor of God" (Eph. 6: 10-20).

CHAPTER 16

The Letter to Philippi

No church gave Paul more satisfaction than did the one he founded at Philippi. In Thessalonica many Christians, stirred up concerning the end of the world, became idle and meddlesome. In Galatia the churches were so near to giving up the central Christian faith in God's free grace that Paul had to write sternly. In Corinth quarrels and moral problems hurt the church and troubled Paul. In Colossae the tendency to make Christ only one helper on the way to God blurred the central and sufficient role of Christ. But in Philippi, while friction occurred, nothing dangerous seems to have threatened the church, and Paul found joy and satisfaction in their Christian faith and friendship.

The First Days of the Church

Philippi was the first place Paul worked in Europe. Crossing from Troas and landing at Neapolis (Acts 16: 11), he went on nine miles to Philippi and began to preach. Some Jews must have lived there; Jewish influence was evidently a danger when he wrote (Phil. 3: 2), but, oddly enough, no synagogue is clearly mentioned. The first Sabbath, Paul went outside the city to a place by the River Gangites, to a Jewish "place of prayer" (Acts 16: 13). A synagogue might be so described, but since Paul found only a group of women present, and it took ten men to form a synagogue, what Paul found seems to have been an informal meeting for worship and friendship.

Any opportunity to preach was welcome to Paul. And here, as elsewhere, it had results. The Acts tells us the name of only one convert. This was Lydia, a Gentile businesswoman from Thyatira in Asia Minor, who had been interested in the Jewish faith (Acts 16: 14). She believed, and so did her household. Later the jailer and his household believed (Acts 16: 34). But that many others also believed in Christ is clear. When Paul had to leave Philippi, he left behind a church, strong enough to send him gifts to support him in his work at Thessalonica (Phil. 4: 16).

There is a hint that women were prominent in this church. It was to them that Paul first preached. In his letter he mentions two women who had been active with him in the work of the gospel (Phil. 4: 2, 3). This, however, does not mean that women were the officers of the church. The "overseers and ministers" mentioned in Phil. 1: 1 were undoubtedly men.

How long Paul stayed in Philippi we do not know. But finally an unexpected crisis led him to leave. A slave girl with an evil spirit and an uncanny ability to utter supposedly divine messages annoyed Paul and his companions, until the apostle, in the name of Jesus Christ, amazingly restored her mental balance and health. The slave girl's owners stirred up a riot against Paul. They hid their real motive, loss of income from the girl's fortunetelling, by a loud appeal to Roman patriotism. Beaten and jailed, Paul and his companion Silas were even locked in the stocks. That night, however, an earthquake loosened both the prison doors and the stocks. The jailer, thinking that the prisoners had escaped, was ready to kill himself. Paul stopped him and used the occasion to lead him to faith in Christ. When the prisoners were released the next day, they required an apology because, though Roman citizens, they had been beaten without a trial. They visited and encouraged the church, which gathered in Lydia's house for this final worship and meeting with them. Then Paul and Silas left the city (Acts 16: 16-40).

The Church Sends Gifts to Paul

The Philippians did not forget Paul. They knew that he did not ask gifts from the church in which he was working. So to help him in his preaching at Thessalonica they twice sent him money (Phil. 4: 16). Perhaps Phil. 4: 15 means that they sent other gifts after that. But then, though their interest continued, they were not able to send further help, and Paul does not blame them (Phil. 4: 10).

Some years later, Paul was in prison (Phil. 1: 12-14). It is not certain where this was. One suggestion is Ephesus, but no solid evidence supports it. The references to the "praetorian guard" and to "those of Caesar's household" (Phil. 1: 13; 4: 22) seem on the whole to point to Rome, where Paul spent two years in prison (Acts 28: 30).

Hearing that Paul was in prison and in need, the Philippians did two things to show Christian friendship. They sent one of their own group, Epaphroditus, to stay with Paul and do all he could to make Paul's life comfortable. By Epaphroditus they also sent a gift to supply the wants of Paul.

The plan did not work out as they had intended. Epaphroditus became seriously sick, and for a time was in danger of death. When he won the fight, and began to recover strength, Paul decided it was not right to keep him longer. The man was weak from his almost fatal sickness. He wanted to go home; probably he felt that now he was more of a hindrance than a help to Paul, and that he could get well more rapidly at home. It was agreed that he should return to Philippi.

Why Paul Wrote

This gave Paul a way to send the Philippians a letter. There were several reasons that led him to write. He wanted to make it clear why Epaphroditus was returning. He did not want his friend, who had suffered such illness while caring for him, to be rebuked or belittled by the Philippians for not staying with

Paul. By a letter he could say why Epaphroditus was returning, and explain that he was sending him home (Phil. 2: 25-30).

Paul also wanted to thank the Philippians for the gift they had sent him. Up to this time, it seems, he had not been able to do so. Now he could send his thanks for their thoughtfulness and kind action (Phil. 4: 10-20).

At the same time he could tell his friends how things were going with him, and what prospects he had for the future. He could make it plain that not even imprisonment had clouded his spirit or broken his faith (cf. Phil. 1: 12-26).

Then, too, the Philippian church showed some signs of pride and division, and this troubled him. It cannot have caused a deep split, for Paul shows too much joy and confidence in this church. But it was a danger, and Paul wanted to correct it before it became worse (Phil. 4: 2).

Like all Paul's churches, the Philippian church needed further instruction. Some needed to be warned not to regard Jewish practices as necessary for salvation; for example, outside teachers were saying that circumcision was required (Phil. 3: 2). Others had to be warned against those who flouted all moral standards and discipline, indulged fleshly appetites, and claimed that God's free grace excused them from pure and upright living (Phil. 3: 17-19). It was with all these points in mind that Paul, about A.D. 62 or 63, dictated the letter.

Local Church Officers

The opening address has one new feature. Paul refers to the "bishops and deacons" (Phil. 1: 1). Perhaps he does so because they had a leading part in sending the gift to him. In his earlier letters no definite local officers have been mentioned. We hear of prophets, teachers, and others who have a part in leading the Church (I Cor. 12: 28; Eph. 4: 11). General references to leading men occur (I Thess. 5: 12; I Cor. 16: 16, 18). But names of offices are not given. No fixed and universal system had been established.

Even when the names of definite officers at Philippi are given, we must not be misled by the modern meaning of the terms. The so-called "bishops" are "overseers," as the Greek word means. Since there were several of them in the one church at Philippi, they were not like the bishops of large areas that we know today, but were more like our local pastors and elders. The duties of the "deacons," or "ministers," are not clearly stated. But the Church was developing its organization to lead, govern, and serve its life.

Paul's Joy and Hope

Paul's thanks for the faith and friendship of this church are hearty and warm (Phil. 1:3-11), and he prays for its growth in faith. The note of joy rings in every chapter, not only in the thanksgivings, but in passages where the words "joy" and "rejoice" occur. Sixteen times Paul uses this Greek noun or verb.

Paul hastens to speak with courage and hope concerning his lot in prison (Phil. 1: 12-30). Even though a prisoner, he has been able to make the gospel known among the soldiers who guard him, and among many other groups.

The situation has its dark side. Some of the Roman leaders are not friendly to him, and envy guides their preaching. Paul is too greathearted to let this crush his spirit. He is glad that the gospel is widely preached, and he trusts that in spite of all hostility and envy he yet will live to revisit the Philippians. He is willing to die; old and worn as he is, he feels that it would be a release to die and go to closer fellowship with Christ. But it is not his wish that counts; if he lives, he can continue to help the Philippians, and that he hopes to do. But whether he lives or dies, they must stand firm in faith.

Appeal for Unity

In that faith they should also stand united. To promote unity each Christian must have humility and not "think of himself more highly than he ought to think" (Rom. 12: 3). They must all remember the example of the humble life and suffering of Christ, and how God honored him by making him Lord of all things (Phil. 2: 1-11). Knowing that God is at work in them, they on their part must live in loyal harmony. They should continue to be an example to others. This will enable Paul to rejoice both now and at the last day (Phil. 2: 12-18).

After telling of his plan to send Timothy, his trusted helper, to them soon, and explaining why Epaphroditus is returning (Phil. 2: 19-30), he warns against Jewish legalistic perversions of the gospel. Jewish descent and Jewish rites are not essential. Paul himself was a Jew of good birth, zealous life, and high outward attainment, but he had dropped all trust in these things because what he needed was the forgiveness and power of God, which he found in Christ his risen Lord. He sets his mind on one thing, to carry out God's full purpose for him in the Christian life. The Philippians should do the same (Phil. 3: 1-16).

The early Gentile Christians had to choose which leaders they were to follow. For practical purposes they had to imitate either Paul or his opponents. So he appeals in more than one letter for his churches to imitate him (Phil. 3: 17). He does not speak out of jealousy, but because others try to mislead the Philippians. There are those whose "god is the belly"; they live lives of self-indulgence and immorality, thinking that these things do not affect the spiritual life or that God will forgive any amount of sin. Since we ask God to bless our entire self and to give it perfect form at the end, we should give our entire lives now in full dedication and pure living. Immoral indulgence has no place in the life of Christians (Phil. 3: 18-21).

Another threat to unity is a quarrel between two women in the church. They should be helped to return to mutual friendship (Phil. 4: 1-3). Paul evidently expects a short appeal to end this trouble. He at once goes on to urge the readers to rejoice.

The Christian life is a grateful, happy life, in which trust in God and confident prayer are natural (Phil. 4: 4-7).

People become what they think. This is a terrible thought in our day, when the level of entertainment in newspapers, radio, television, and social life is so shallow. But it is true. Paul knew this. So he urged his friends to think of the good, true, and lovely things. They should not merely think about them, but also practice them, as they have seen him doing (Phil. 4: 8, 9).

Paul and His Friends

Now he thanks them for the gift. The way he does so may seem surprising. At first it almost seems that he did not care whether they sent him a gift or not; he could get along without it. But he did need the gift, and he is grateful for it. He just does not want them to think that his happiness depends only or chiefly on physical conditions. He has lived years with a "thorn . . . in the flesh" (II Cor. 12: 7); he has endured physical hardship and torture; he has been cold and hungry. But these things have never been able to defeat him. His faith and his work for Christ mean vastly more to him than do physical comfort and safety, and he wants his readers to see that this must always be true of a Christian. So he thanks them in such a way that physical supplies will not seem the chief thing in life. But he thanks them warmly, rejoices that they have remembered him, recalls with gratitude their earlier gifts, and assures them that God's blessing will be with such kindly givers (Phil. 4: 10-20).

Among those who send Christian greetings (Phil. 4: 21-23) are "those of Caesar's household." They may have been slaves or servants; we do not know. But one thing is clear: the gospel was spreading and reaching into the circle of those who served Caesar. The immoral and cruel Nero was on the throne. The apostle Paul was in prison and before long would die. But the future was with the faith of Paul; it was better to share his faith than to imitate the immoral pleasures of the emperor. Christ is the true Lord, and the Christian life is the true life.

A Life Gladly Given to Christ

This is a strange letter to come from a prison. It is full of courage, and superior to the outward situation. It breathes determination to go on with Christian work in spite of persecution and envy. It is marked by joy and gratitude to God for the privilege of preaching the gospel. It expresses deep love for Christian friends and joy in their faith and growth.

In prison or free, Paul lives for Christ. He points to him as the object of faith, as the example of humility and unique greatness, and as the Lord of his people. Paul's one aim is to serve Christ and fulfill Christ's purpose for his life. "One thing I do, forgetting the things which are behind, and stretching forward to the things which are before, I press on toward the goal unto the prize of the high calling of God in Christ Jesus." (Phil. 3: 13, 14.)

Reading Hints: In reading Philippians, list the things for which Paul gives thanks to God. What things at Philippi make him rejoice and what weaknesses does he see?

Passages to Study: Christian humility (Phil. 2: 1-4); the humility and glory of Christ the Lord (Phil. 2: 5-11); the humility and goal of Paul (Phil. 3: 4-16); Christian thinking (Phil. 4: 8).

Verses Worth Remembering: Phil. 1: 21; 2: 12, 13; 3: 13, 14; 4: 4, 6, 8, 13.

CHAPTER 17

Three Letters to Pastors

FAMOUS MEN deserve credit for what they achieve. Yet without loyal friends and assistants they could never make the great record they do.

Such loyal helpers keep appearing in the story of Paul. Only rarely was he left alone, and then for but a short time (Acts 17: 15; I Thess. 3: 1, 2). Usually one or more of his assistants will join him in writing a letter, and when no one is with him to help him in his work, that is only because he has sent these trusted men to aid churches in other cities.

TIMOTHY AND TITUS

Two of the most faithful helpers Paul had were Timothy and Titus. We hear most often of Timothy. In six letters Paul names Timothy as one of the writers. Paul himself dictates the letter, but he names his helper to show that he has confidence in Timothy and that they stand together in their work.

Paul had converted Timothy at Lystra. On his second great missionary journey he took Timothy with him when he left Lystra (Acts 16: 1-3), and from then on Timothy became Paul's constant helper. Perhaps he was timid at times (I Cor. 16: 10, 11), but he was loyal and faithful, and Paul sent him on journeys to such important churches as those at Thessalonica and Corinth (I Thess. 3: 1, 2; I Cor. 4: 17). He was ready to share imprisonment with Paul to be near him and help him (Phil. 1: 1; Col. 1: 1; Philemon 1). Like Paul, he was "genuinely anxious" for the welfare of the churches; in fact, Paul can say of him: "Timothy's worth you know, how as a son with a father he has served with me in the gospel" (Phil. 2: 19-22). At one time Paul left him to lead the church at Ephesus (I Tim. 1: 3).

Titus, a Gentile Christian, never appears in the book of The Acts. Since Paul calls him "my true child in a common faith" (Titus 1: 4), it is probable that the apostle converted him. He went with Paul to the conference held at Jerusalem to decide whether Gentile Christians had to keep the law to be saved (Gal. 2: 3). He helped Paul at Corinth in particular. To this church he carried letters; he led it back to loyalty to Paul when it had rebelled; he guided the gathering of its collection for the poor Christians in Jerusalem (II Cor. 7: 5-16; 8: 16-24; 12: 18). Later he worked in Crete, joined Paul during a winter stay at Nicopolis in Greece, and was sent on a mission to Dalmatia, northwest of Macedonia (Titus 1: 5; 3: 12; II Tim. 4: 10).

Letters to Pastors

To these two trusted helpers of Paul are addressed the three letters that we are now to study. The first and second letters to Timothy and the one to Titus belong together. They are the only letters addressed to traveling helpers of Paul. In what they say and how they say it they are quite similar. They speak to leaders of the Church, and describe especially the character and abilities that local leaders must have. They warn against false ideas and practices, and point out the mistakes that leaders must avoid.

Obviously these letters do not speak only of the duties of Timothy and Titus. They have in mind the many leaders of local churches. A single word at the close of each letter shows that they speak to these many others as well. In the closing prayer, "Grace be with you," the Greek word for "you" is plural. So it is clear that the letters were not private notes for only one person, but were written also to guide the thinking and action of other Christian leaders, both those who worked with Timothy and Titus and those who carried on their work after them.

Christians today call these three letters the Pastoral Epistles. That is because they state the duties and describe the character of pastors and other local church leaders. What do they have to say?

"I Have Finished the Race"

These are not the letters of a beginner in the work of Christ. They are rather the words of a veteran missionary, and they speak of the work of the Church in many Roman cities and provinces. The gospel has spread; the Church has grown; years of fruitful preaching have passed. The apostle himself speaks as an old man who sees the end of his active career drawing near. "I am already on the point of being sacrificed; the time of my departure has come. I have fought the good fight, I have finished the race, I have kept the faith" (II Tim. 4: 6, 7).

It is clear from I Timothy and Titus that Paul has been in Ephesus and Crete and has a plan to spend the winter in Nicopolis, which was probably located in northwestern Greece (I Tim. 1: 3; Titus 1: 5; 3: 12). But in II Timothy he is again in prison; he has already appeared in court once (II Tim. 4: 16). He still speaks for Christ by letter, by messenger, and by the witness he gives before his judges, but his ministry is drawing to a close.

"Hold Firm to the Sure Word"

What will become of the Church? Will it stay true to the gospel? Only if its leaders constantly guide it in straight thinking and correct teaching about the way to live. We sometimes hear it said that it makes no difference what we believe, just so we do what is right. This is nonsense. We become what we think; action is shaped by what we believe and dwell on in our thoughts. False ideas are always popping up, and the Church to help its people must constantly teach what faith in God and Christ means, how Christians should live together, and what their Christian task is.

That is why Paul always wanted the leaders and the Church to "hold firm to the sure word" of Christian truth (Titus 1: 9). Many harmful ideas were threatening the Christians. Some were urging the adoption of Jewish rites (Titus 1: 10, 14). These letters to pastors give a place to law: it can warn against wrong and command good things; but to trust in ceremonies and in legalistic rules as the way to be saved is to forget the grace of God. Some were thinking that "genealogies" or family trees of angelic beings should be learned, and that the way to God could be found through these helpers (I Tim. 1: 4; 4: 7). There were quarrels and disputes, and many took pride in their own pet ideas (I Tim. 6: 20; II Tim. 2: 14, 23; Titus 3: 9). Many tried to win salvation by ascetic practices: they forbade marriage, tortured the body, and banned the eating of meat (I Tim. 4: 3, 8).

Greed and love of money were ruining Christian brotherhood (I Tim. 6: 9, 10, 17-19), and so was idle gossip (I Tim. 5: 13). Arrogant, inhuman action threatened to increase (II Tim. 3: 2-5). Gluttony and drunkenness were ready to claim victims, and love of the evil world had already hurt the Church (I Tim. 3: 3, 8; II Tim. 4: 10; Titus 1: 12).

Against all these false ideas, these clever attempts of men to save themselves, these selfish quarrels and actions, the Pastoral Epistles stand firm for the gospel of Christ. It is the trustworthy message of how God saves men through Christ and builds them up in new and wholesome life. "When the goodness and loving kindness of God our Savior appeared, he saved us, not because of deeds done by us in righteousness, but in virtue of his own mercy, by the washing of regeneration and renewal in the Holy Spirit, which he poured out upon us richly through Jesus Christ our Savior" (Titus 3: 4-6). It is

God who saves us; it is his power that enables us to live good lives; through Christ and the Spirit we can become what we should be.

"Be Rich in Good Deeds"

Because God gives the Christians such power, they must show its effect in their lives. Jesus gave a simple but terrifying test by which to tell whether Christian leaders and people are really true to him: "You will know them by their fruits" (Matt. 7: 16, 20). So, too, the Pastoral Epistles often insist on good deeds.

It is true that the gospel offers free forgiveness to sinful men. We do not earn our place with God. That is a gift, which we receive through faith in Christ. But for this gift the Christian is grateful, and in grateful faith he accepts and does the will of God. By God's help he can do good deeds, and his daily life should show this fruit of faith.

So we read that the Christian and especially the leaders are to be "rich in good deeds," "ready for any good work," "zealous for good deeds" (I Tim. 6: 18; II Tim. 2: 21; Titus 2: 14). "Let our people learn to apply themselves to good deeds, so as to help cases of urgent need, and not to be unfruitful" (Titus 3: 14). They must never be like those who "profess to know God, but they deny him by their deeds" (Titus 1: 16).

"Fulfill Your Ministry"

The Church needs able leaders, and it is of them that the Pastoral Epistles have most to say. What qualities in leaders do these letters stress? They emphasize sincere faith, dedicated life, and faithful service. No long list of special talents occurs; ability to teach is the main gift mentioned. But the leader must be honest, gentle, free from greed and quarrelsomeness, steady, self-disciplined, and with a home that gives a good witness for his faith. No special talents can take the place of these qualities. The leader must keep learning, especially from

Scripture (II Tim. 3: 14-17). His task is to give both good teaching and a good example, and he must accept and endure any hardship that comes (I Tim. 4: 11-16; II Tim. 2: 3; 4: 2).

Who are these leaders? In part the instruction is given to Timothy and Titus as examples of all church leaders. But these letters pay special attention to local church officers. One such officer is the "overseer" or "bishop"—he is also called "elder" (I Tim. 3: 1-7; Titus 1: 5-9). In Titus 1: 7 it is clear that the "overseer" or "bishop" is an elder. The word "for" shows that the "bishop" of which Titus 1: 7 speaks is one of the same persons that the preceding sentence called "elders." Just so, Paul in Acts 20: 17, 28 calls the elders "overseers" or "bishops." The Greek word he uses in Acts 20: 28 is the one that in Titus 1: 7 is translated "bishop." These "overseers" or elders are to rule the local congregation, and some of them are to take the lead in preaching and teaching (I Tim. 5: 17).

There are also deacons (I Tim. 3: 8-13). They must be men of true faith and good character. Since they handle funds and care for the poor, they must be honest and reliable. In fact, more than once these letters warn of the dangers of wealth; deacons are not the only ones who must make and use money in a Christian way.

A special class are the elderly widows who have no family to care for them. They are to be enrolled in a special group and supported by the church, and in return are to give faithful service to those who need their help (I Tim. 5: 3-16). For this service they must be women of highest character.

Where Do These Letters Fit in Paul's Life?

When were the Pastoral Epistles written? One fact is clear. They do not fit into the story that the book of The Acts tells. According to I Tim. 1: 3, Paul left Timothy at Ephesus when he went north to Macedonia. But in The Acts, the one time that Paul thus went north, he sent Timothy on ahead (Acts 19: 22). In II Tim. 1: 8, 16, Paul is again a prisoner, and he is or has been in Rome. But this is not the imprisonment of which The Acts tells, for in II Timothy Paul says he left Trophimus sick in Miletus (II Tim. 4: 20), while we know from Acts 21: 29 that on the trip that led to Paul's arrest and voyage to Rome, Trophimus went with Paul to Jerusalem. Again, Paul says he left Titus in Crete to continue the work he had begun there, and he plans to winter at Nicopolis (Titus 1: 5; 3: 12). Nothing in The Acts indicates that Paul ever went to Crete. Even when he sailed past it as a prisoner, he was not able to stop and preach. Nor does The Acts ever suggest that Paul wintered at Nicopolis.

Thus the Pastoral Epistles contain details that do not fit into the story of The Acts. Of course we do not know all that Paul did in those years, but too many details fail to fit. If Paul wrote these letters, he must have done so after the period that The Acts covers. That is, he must have been acquitted and freed at Rome. Then he must have traveled in the East again, worked in Crete, revisited Ephesus, gone from there to Macedonia, and wintered in Nicopolis—or planned to do so. During these travels he could have written I Timothy and Titus. Later he must have been arrested again and taken to Rome, where II Timothy could have been written while he was waiting for trial.

But was Paul released from prison? Nothing in The Acts hints that he was. Paul even tells the elders of the Ephesian church that they will never see him again (Acts 20: 25, 38). Does Luke imply that Paul was condemned and put to death at Rome after being a prisoner there two years (Acts 28: 30)? This is not certain. If Luke wrote The Acts before Paul was tried, he could not tell how the trial came out. If he wrote later, as is probable, he told no more because his purpose was not to write a complete life of Paul but to tell how the gospel reached Rome.

Though Luke tells us no more, an ancient tradition reports that Paul was released about A.D. 63 and did further mission work as far west as Spain. This story we hear first from Clement of Rome, who in a letter about A.D. 96 implies that Paul went to Spain. But a difficulty arises here. The Pastoral Epistles never hint that Paul went west to Spain, and Clement gives no hint that Paul went back to the East as the Pastoral Epistles imply he did. Can we say that he first went to Spain, and then back to the East, where he worked, wrote letters, and finally was arrested again and taken to Rome? If so, the martyrdom of Paul could be placed at the close of this second Roman imprisonment (A.D. 64 or 67).

Did Paul Really Write These Letters?

Before we conclude that Paul wrote these three letters in the period after The Acts closes, we must face other questions they raise. In some ways they are not like other letters Paul wrote. They repeatedly insist on "sound teaching" (II Tim. 4: 3). Over a dozen passages stress the need for correct belief and instruction. Paul certainly taught and defended the truth. But this repeated explicit emphasis on correct teaching and right belief is new.

In a similar way these letters stress the necessity of "good deeds." Again there are over a dozen passages with this demand. Paul was quick to rebuke moral failures and inaction, but such a frequent use of the phrase "good deeds" has no parallel in his other letters.

Another new feature is the careful statement of the qualities local church leaders must have. In writing to churches, he says little of officers and their abilities. Apart from Phil. 1: 1, he speaks mainly of the Spirit-guided prophets, teachers, and healers (I Cor. 12: 28; Eph. 4: 11). But here we read of definite local officers and their qualifications (I Tim. 3: 1-13; 5: 17; Titus 1: 5-9).

Then, too, the Greek words and the style of writing in the Pastoral Epistles are quite different from what we find in the letters Paul wrote to churches. Could Paul have written so differently? Would a man in old age change his vocabulary and style so much?

Such difficulties might tempt us to decide that Paul had nothing to do with the writing of the Pastoral Epistles. But the personal statements about his ministry and the details about his travels and companions are not fiction. They come from Paul. He speaks in these letters.

So one of two things happened. Perhaps, toward the end of his life, Paul determined to stress correct teaching, insist strongly on good works, and give more definite attention to local church leaders. But he did not dictate the letters word for word; he let a helper or trusted secretary put his ideas in final form. Or possibly Paul wrote shorter letters that a companion or admirer later expanded into the present form the letters have. Such a later expansion would have applied what Paul had written to conditions that rose after his death. But with either view, these letters owe their basic gospel to Paul and they express his personal testimony to the truth of the Christian message.

Let the Church Stand Fast

In the Pastoral Epistles we see the Church beginning to take more definite form. At first, when all the disciples were Jews, they lived within Judaism. They worshiped in the Temple and synagogue, and did not seek to build a separate organization. But as the Church became largely Gentile, it more and more had to find its own ways of worshiping and living together. It became a separate group, and had to take a firm and independent stand in the Empire. It could not compromise with paganism, though it did show its good will toward all men, and it prayed for all rulers and governors (I Tim. 2: 1-4).

The worship of the Church developed. The Scripture had its important place (II Tim. 3: 14-17). It seems that hymns began to be composed. Possibly I Tim. 3: 16 preserves one such hymn; at least it shows us how the Church was forming statements of its central faith. The words, "Faithful is the saying," or, "The saying is sure," occur five times; they point to statements of faith that were often repeated by Christians and so were becoming well known (I Tim. 1: 15; 3: 1; 4: 9; II Tim. 2: 11; Titus 3: 8).

When we have a good thing we want to keep it. This is the idea that controls the Pastoral Epistles. Since in the gospel and the Christian life we have the greatest gift life can offer, since in Christ we have the right center of life, let us keep it. We should think rightly about it. We should act in loyalty to Jesus Christ. Let us make the life and leadership of the Church ever more worthy and faithful. "Guard what has been entrusted to you" (I Tim. 6: 20).

Reading Hints: As you read these letters, see what they say about:

Paul's travels, friends, and work (I Tim. 1: 3, 12-16, 20; 3: 14, 15; II Tim. 1: 3-6, 8, 11, 12, 15-18; 2: 9; 4: 6-21; Titus 1: 5; 3: 12-14).

Paul's gospel (I Tim. 1: 15; 2: 5-7; 3: 16; 4: 10; 6: 13-16; II Tim. 1: 8-14; 2: 8, 11; 3: 16, 17; Titus 2: 11-14; 3: 3-8).

Church officers (I Tim. 3: 1-13; 5: 17; Titus 1: 5-9).

What traits should a Christian leader have? What faults should he avoid? Of what false ideas should he beware?

CHAPTER 18

The Letter to the Hebrews

IT COST to serve God in New Testament days. Misguided men beheaded John the Baptist, crucified Jesus, stoned Stephen, "killed James the brother of John with the sword," and, according to ancient tradition, made martyrs of Peter and Paul. To be denounced, beaten, imprisoned, and driven from synagogue and city was nothing rare or unusual. It is true that the New Testament often rings with words of thanksgiving and joy. But this is not the speech of pampered men; it is the triumph of faith over hardship and danger. It costs to be true to the Christian faith and task.

Was every Christian ready to endure such treatment? The fact that Judas betrayed Jesus reminds us that some started out as disciples and failed to stay strong and faithful. It was not easy to stand forth and speak up for Christ when to do so brought danger. The courage and loyalty of some weakened and crumpled when tested.

"Let Us Hold Fast Our Confession"

To a group thus tempted to give up their faith the Letter to the Hebrews was written. They were not mere weaklings. Once before they had undergone severe trial. They had been denounced and their property seized. But they had stood fast. Not only had they been true to their faith under attack; some who could have escaped attention had courageously shown sympathy and helpfulness to persecuted fellow Christians

(Heb. 10: 32-34). But continued trial was proving a strain. They had not given up their faith, but their courage was wavering. Their "drooping hands" and "weak knees" (Heb. 12: 12) did not promise well for the future.

This letter strongly urges them to hold fast. The writer is either a member or at least a close friend of the group he addresses. He has been with them before, and though now absent, he looks forward to seeing them again (Heb. 13: 19, 23). But they need to hear at once what he has to say. So he writes this "word of exhortation" (Heb. 13: 22), and sends it for them to read aloud when they meet to worship God and encourage one another.

Is It a Letter?

Is this really a letter? It does not begin like one. Instead, it opens with a formal, impressive statement of central Christian truth. Yet at the end we find the tone of a letter, with personal greetings and bits of news.

All this is because the author knows that what he writes will be read aloud when these Christians meet. It will take the place of the sermon or appeal that the writer would give if he could be present. So he begins by presenting the gospel truth on which he will base his appeal. But since he writes from a distance, it is in effect a letter, and he ends it with greetings and items of news such as a letter contains.

A Faith Too Important to Surrender

His appeal combines instruction and warning. The Christian gospel is the true message of full and final salvation. The readers cannot give it up without immeasurable loss.

God had spoken to men before, through the Old Testament prophets. But now in Christ his Son, the central figure of history, he has revealed himself most fully. He has redeemed men from their sins and offers them now the one effective salvation. Thus through the unique Son, who is superior to all

God's creatures and has done what no other could do, God has met man's needs (Heb. 1: 1-4). It would be amazing folly for the readers to turn their backs on the Son and his gifts to men.

Christ Superior to Angels

To show that there is no other worthy object of faith, the writer compares Christ with possible rivals. In New Testament times both Jews and Christians sometimes placed great emphasis on the angels, heavenly beings whom God had created to act as his messengers. So the writer first declares that the Son, who took human form and victoriously endured human struggle and suffering, is superior to the angels. He offers more effective aid to men and has greater honor with God than they do (Heb. 1: 5 to 2: 18). To us it seems strange to regard angels as real rivals to Christ, but that was just what happened. In fact, some men thought that the human life and struggle of Jesus put him on an even lower plane than angels held. But this writer, looking to the moral victory of Jesus (Heb. 2: 18; 4: 15) and to his power to help men to face and master life, knows that no angel of God can challenge the supreme place of Christ.

The purpose of this letter is intensely practical. It seeks to help the readers to hold fast in their faith. So at each stage of the argument the writer includes an earnest warning that men cannot slight God's great gift in Christ without eternal loss. Here he warns against drifting away from "such a great salvation." Men can lose the best that life offers, not only by deliberately turning from it, but also by neglecting it and letting it slip quietly away, until the damage is done. Against such careless loss of the best this first warning is given (Heb. 2: 1-4).

Christ Superior to Moses and Joshua

How does Jesus compare with Moses and Joshua? Moses led the people of Israel out of Egypt, and God gave him the law to give to them. Joshua later brought this people into the Promised Land, where it could become a united nation and have a common religious life. But the greatest leader is Christ. He, the Son of God, is superior to Moses and Joshua, not only in personal worth, but also in ability to give to those who follow him a true spiritual home and place of blessed rest. He leads his people out of the wilderness wandering of earth's trials and into a life of perfect fellowship with God (Heb. 3: 1 to 4: 13).

Hence the warning: Beware of unbelief and disobedience (Heb. 3: 7 to 4: 13). Put full faith in Christ and be faithful to him whatever comes. In this warning the word "today" keeps recurring. Now is the time to believe and make sure that this rest, this home with God, will always be ours. A calloused heart is fatal; hear and keep faith with God now, today.

Christ the Great High Priest

Another important figure in Jewish religion in New Testament times was the high priest. His responsibilities for carrying out the sacrifices in the Temple are described in the Old Testament book of Leviticus. How do Christ and the Jewish high priest compare (Heb. 4: 14 to 7: 28)? Here the writer's great interest in the priestly system of Leviticus begins to show, and it shapes most of the rest of the letter. Among the priests the high priest was the outstanding leader. He performed his special ministry on the Day of Atonement. Every day, according to the law, an appointed priest went into the Holy Place of the Tabernacle to care for the lamps and make the daily offering. But one day a year, on the Day of Atonement, the high priest went alone into the Most Holy Place (Lev., ch. 16). Since he was but an imperfect, sinful man, he had to go twice. The first time he took the blood of a sacrifice offered to cover his own sins. Then he was fit and ready to return and offer the blood sacrifice for the sins of the people of Israel. This act was the supreme ministry of the priestly system.

But Christ is superior to the high priest. He was without sin (Heb. 4: 15), so did not have to offer a sacrifice for himself before he was fit to minister for others. He had indeed lived a life of moral struggle "in the days of his flesh." He had faced and met death to be true to his task. But in trial he had been victorious; he can sympathize with men's trials and he is worthy to act for their salvation (Heb. 2: 18; 4: 15).

In a curious way the writer compares Jesus the Son with Melchizedek, the ancient king of Salem, mentioned in Gen. 14: 18-20. The Old Testament does not mention Melchizedek's father, mother, birth, or death. So the author of this letter, taking his cue from Ps. 110: 4, interprets the omission as a symbol of the eternal existence of the Son. In particular, now that the Son has entered the heavenly sanctuary, he is forever with God, and does not have to be replaced every generation, as do the mortal high priests of Israel. He is the eternal and only perfect high priest, and is always seeking from the Father the gifts that will bless his followers.

Hence the warning: Do not be sluggish and indifferent in spirit. Grow up to spiritual maturity and be faithful to the end. The writer sees no hope for people who have known the blessings of Christian life and yet turn their backs on Christ. So he warns his readers to stand up under trial and keep on doing good works (Heb. 5: 11 to 6: 12).

Christ the Perfect Sacrifice for Sin

Not only is Christ more worthy than the sinful high priests of Israel, but the sacrifice he offers is more effective (Heb., chs. 8 to 10). Indeed, he offers the one effective sacrifice. The blood of animals cannot take away sin (Heb. 10: 4). But when the sinless Son of God offers himself on behalf of men, that is a perfect and acceptable offering. The tabernacle in which he offers this one perfect offering is the true tabernacle in heaven (Heb. 9: 24). He takes his blood, shed at his death on the cross, and offers it in heaven, just as the high priest takes the blood from the altar in the Tabernacle court and presents it in the Most Holy Place.

What does the writer intend to say when he compares Christ's death with the priestly offerings? Just this: Christ willingly offered his life to help sinful men. God acted through his Son to save them. This action was fully effective and opened the way to God. Those who put their trust in Christ receive forgiveness of their sins and Christ is their constant representative, or high priest, in the presence of God (Heb. 9: 24). Thus the priestly system on earth is outmoded; it is only the symbol of Christ's effective sacrifice and constant ministry for us.

Hence another warning: To sin willfully after receiving knowledge of this truth, to give up faith in Christ who has done and is doing everything man needs to be saved and blessed, is not only the greatest possible foolishness; it is the sure way to judgment and disaster. Let the Christian beware lest he fall away and suffer such a ruinous judgment (Heb. 10: 26-31).

Thus the Christian faith is the one true faith, the one effective way to God and eternal life. Not angels, not Moses or Joshua, not the high priests or the sacrifices they offer, but Christ and Christ alone is the adequate source of help and hope. The readers rightly held fast when they were persecuted before; they should hold fast now (Heb. 10: 32-39).

Faith Includes Faithfulness

To help the readers to hold to that faith, the writer describes it and points out in Scripture great examples of faith in Israel. True faith always includes perseverance, and perseverance is what the readers now must show (Heb., chs. 11; 12). Like those heroes of faith, "let us also lay aside every weight, and sin which clings so closely, and let us run with perseverance the race that is set before us, looking to Jesus the pioneer and perfecter of our faith, who for the joy that was set before him endured the cross, despising the shame, and is seated at the right hand of the throne of God" (Heb. 12: 1, 2).

To this appeal is attached another earnest warning. God has spoken; he has acted in Christ. The God who offers every needed gift in Christ is also the God who will judge those who slight his gifts. Christians must not spurn and toss aside their priceless privilege; that would mean their ruin (Heb. 12: 18-29).

In the New Testament faith is always related to life. So here the reason the writer stresses the unique and effective work of Christ is to induce the readers to hold fast to their faith and be true to it in daily life. Hospitality, brotherly good will, sympathy with the unfortunate, purity of life, freedom from greed, respect for good leaders, prayer, loyalty to the group, and above all to Christ—these are Christian duties he emphasizes (Heb. 13: 1-19). He closes his letter with friendly words and prayer which show how confident he is that the readers will heed what he has said (Heb. 13: 20-25).

The Author and Readers

Who wrote this letter? Does it not say that Paul did? No. Though some English Bibles name Paul in the heading, that heading was added long after the letter was written. Do not all ancient Christian writers say Paul wrote it? No. The ancient Christians were not certain. Some said Paul was the author; one leader said Barnabas; others had no idea who wrote it.

Is the wording and style that of Paul? No. The Greek of Hebrews is definitely not like the Greek of Paul's letters. Does the manner of thinking parallel Paul's? No. The priestly system in the Old Testament interests the writer of Hebrews; Paul centers attention on its legal system and the note of faith he finds there.

No one can say who wrote Hebrews. It was not Paul. The idea that Barnabas did has nothing to support it. The theory, which Luther favored, that Apollos was the author is only a guess. Other views, that Silas or Luke or Priscilla and Aquila wrote the letter, lack solid evidence to support them. It is a great and instructive writing by a gifted and inspired Christian leader whose name we can never determine and do not need to know.

Where he wrote, and where his readers lived, is not clear. Heb. 13: 24 may mean that he addresses a specific church group in Italy, and he is elsewhere. Others from Italy are with him, and send greetings back home. If this is correct, the readers may have lived in Rome.

The date of writing is not certain. Nero, emperor in A.D. 54-68, persecuted Christians in Rome in the last years of his reign; so also, it appears, did Domitian (A.D. 81-96). Perhaps at other times the Christians of Italy had to suffer. This letter was written after its readers had passed through one period of suffering in "the former days" (Heb. 10: 32). Those "former days" could have been about A.D. 64, when Nero maliciously accused the Christians of setting fire to Rome. If so, the letter could not have been written before the late 60's, and quite likely its date was still later, perhaps about A.D. 95, in the reign of the emperor Domitian.

The letter seems to address Jewish Christians. To keep the readers true to the Christian faith, the writer compares it only with possible Old Testament rivals. Christ is superior to the angels of whom the Scripture tells, to Moses and Joshua who led the Hebrews, to the high priest of the Israelite Tabernacle, and to the sacrifices prescribed by the Mosaic law. The author might have argued that Christ is superior to all Gentile philosophers and religions. But he did not. The one group that his argument could completely convince were Jews who had become Christians but now, tired of enduring trials for Christ, might be tempted to go back to Judaism. It appears that the letter went to a Jewish Christian group in Italy, perhaps in the city of Rome.

"Let Us Then with Confidence Draw Near"

The Christian knows that God has fully met his need through Christ. So he surely should not abandon or surrender his privilege. It is Christ who gives men what they need. No one else can do this. Henceforth "let us then with confidence draw near to the throne of grace"; let us look to him, assured that "he always lives to make intercession for them" whom he has already redeemed and now supports in all their need (Heb. 4:16; 7: 25).

The old priesthoods have faded away. Christ did not come to establish a new priesthood without which we cannot reach him. He is still our high priest and we all have free access to him in faith and prayer. The worshiping Church and each praying Christian look directly to him. Each day and for all who will follow, a straight way leads to God through the Son. The central figure of Christian faith and hope is "Jesus Christ . . . the same yesterday and today and forever" (Heb. 13: 8).

Reading Hints: Since the practical purpose of the writer is clearest in the warnings he gives, pay close attention to Heb. 2: 1-4; 3: 7 to 4: 13; 5: 11 to 6: 12; 10: 26-31; 12: 18-29.

Great Passages: God's action through his Son (Heb. 1: 1-4); "made like his brethren," yet victor and "able to help" (Heb. 2: 17, 18; 4: 14-16); the famous chapter on faith (Heb., ch. 11); a great benediction (Heb. 13: 20, 21).

CHAPTER 19

The Letter of James

THE NEW TESTAMENT has a place for stubborn practical sense. Christians are often tempted to pretend to be better than they are. For the health of the Church the false front of such pretense must be torn away. In doing this The Epistle of James has always been helpful.

It does not give the full Christian gospel, and for this reason some Christians have not liked it. For example, Martin Luther, the great leader of the Protestant Reformation, saw that it did not tell clearly how men are saved by the free grace of God. So he ranked it much lower than the letters of Paul and called it "an epistle of straw."

But there is an honored place for this writing that refuses to be impressed by pious pretense unsupported by life. It calls for honest obedience to God in the daily round of duty. This practical teaching is not lacking in other New Testament books, but here it is stated most clearly.

PRACTICAL LESSONS IN CHRISTIAN LIVING

The writer does not have in mind the needs of just one local church. What he says lacks all local color and shows that he sees the faults of the Church at large. Nor does he follow a clear and logical outline. But he knows the pitfalls of life and warns Christians how to avoid them.

He begins with frank words about life's hardship and trials. They can yield a blessing (James 1: 2-15). Sooner or later these difficult times come to all. To live well one must meet them in faith. They can even result in joy. Rightly accepted, with faith in God and with the wisdom he gives to those who ask, they strengthen character. But to blame God, who gives only good and always seeks man's good, is to sin and to miss the meaning of life's trials.

Strong living gives a large place to prayer. He who needs wisdom may have it if he asks God for it in trust (James 1: 5-7). He who humbly draws near to God has the promise that he will be helped (James 4: 7-10). The Christian should build life's plans on God's will (James 4: 15). He should pray in all situations, sad or glad, and pray for others as well as for self (James 5: 13-18).

He should be patient. To fail in this leads to sinful anger and harmful words (James 1: 19-21). It causes hostility between people (James 4: 1-3). It shows unwillingness to accept God's plan and await God's time to act (James 5: 7-11). In fact, such impatience indicates lack of true faith.

To hear the Bible read or to listen to a good sermon is not enough. Hearing without doing is futile (James 1: 22-27). The purpose of the reading and preaching is to direct life. He who does not do what he hears deceives himself; that is the tragedy. He does not deceive others so well, and does not deceive God at all.

The Christian life has no place for "partiality" or "respect of persons" (James 2: 1-13). The Greek word for "partiality" means literally "taking face," that is, treating persons according to their outward appearance and advantages rather than according to their true faith and character. To show such partiality is to sin and split the Church.

To say, "I believe," is far from enough. "Faith without works is dead." If a Christian has faith, real faith, it will show its fruits in action (James 2: 14-26). Here is the outstanding emphasis of the epistle. It never belittles faith, but demands that it be real faith, which shows results in what the believer does. True faith leads to ready helpfulness and personal interest in the welfare of others (James 1: 27). Such helpfulness is an act of religious worship, just as much as is prayer.

The tongue can cause great damage (James 1: 19-21; 3: 1-12). Teachers must take care; they are responsible for what they say in teaching. But all other men too must control the tongue. To say both reverent and sinful things with the same tongue is unnatural and wrong. God requires honest speech. That is why taking an oath is here opposed (James 5: 12). Always tell the truth, so that men need no oath from you to guarantee that your statement is true.

The Christian will not set his heart on pleasures that make him selfishly fight other people (James 4: 1-4). Jealousy, hatred, evil desire, and the driving struggle for riches that makes man forget faith and God while treating other men unjustly—all these are wrong; this search for wealth and luxury is an outstanding enemy of reverent, fair, kindly living (James 4: 2, 13-17; 5: 1-6).

A "Catholic" Epistle

This is not a letter that a postman could deliver. It is one of the so-called "Catholic Epistles." They include seven writings: James, I Peter, II Peter, I John, II John, III John, and Jude. Their name "catholic" implies that they were written to the Church at large; the word here, as in the Apostles' Creed, means "universal." In general, this name fits these writings, although II John and III John refer to more local situations, and are included in this group only because they have the same author as I John.

The word "catholic" fits The Epistle of James. Its writer addresses "the twelve tribes in the dispersion" (James 1: 1). Since the term "the dispersion" was then used to mean all the Jews living dispersed in Gentile lands, this epistle may speak to all Jews, or at least all Christian Jews, who were living outside of Palestine. Or possibly it may address the Christians, the true Israel, who are "dispersed" or scattered in this evil world and whose true home will be in God's Kingdom. Certainly it went to no single church or small group of churches. It addressed either all scattered Jews or all Christians.

It shows no interest in Jewish institutions. It never mentions the Temple, the law's special rites and ceremonies, or the Sabbath. There is also little teaching that only a Christian could give. Jesus is barely mentioned (James 1: 1; 2: 1). His ministry, cross, and resurrection are never recalled. To be sure, the writer knows of them. He calls Jesus "Lord," and his reference to "the coming of the Lord" (James 5: 7, 8) reflects his faith that the risen Lord will return to judge evil and save his people. But direct references to Christ are rare.

Yet many passages recall the teaching of Jesus. God answers men who ask help in prayer (James 1: 5; Matt. 7: 7); the poor will inherit the Kingdom (James 2: 5; Matt. 5: 3; Luke 6: 20); God gives a blessing to peacemakers (James 3: 18; Matt. 5: 9); woe threatens the rich (James 5: 1-6; Luke 6: 24); men are not to use oaths (James 5: 12; Matt. 5: 34-37). This writer knew the teaching of Jesus.

Who Is This James?

The writer describes himself as "a servant of God and of the Lord Jesus Christ" (James 1: 1), that is, he is a Christian working for Christ in the Church. Tradition says that he was James the oldest of four brothers of Jesus (Mark 6: 3; Matt. 13: 55). The four brothers, as Matt. 1: 25 implies, were children of Joseph and Mary, born after the birth of Jesus.

These brothers, we are told (Mark 3: 21; John 7: 5), did not believe in Jesus during his ministry. But he must have had influence upon them, for they became his followers soon after. James was one of those who saw the risen Christ (I Cor. 15: 7), and the brothers all joined the disciples in the Early Church (Acts 1: 14). James soon emerged as a leader, and became prominent in the church at Jerusalem (Acts 12: 17; 15: 13;

21: 18; Gal. 1: 19; 2: 9). In A.D. 62 he was put to death by hostile Jews, but his life had been so upright that other Jews protested this crime.

If this James wrote the epistle, he may have done so quite early. Indeed, some think he wrote it about A.D. 45, so that it was the earliest writing of the New Testament. But since James 2: 14-26 seems to show a knowledge of Paul's preaching and letters, others suppose that James wrote in the early 60's, shortly before his martyr death. If James the brother of the Lord was the author, this later date is most likely to be correct.

Some facts, however, argue that a later Christian was the author. For several generations the ancient Church showed no sign of knowing this epistle. Not until the third century did it begin to be accepted. Why this delay if its date was early and its author was the well-known James? Then, too, the epistle is written in a good Greek style. Could James the Lord's brother write Greek so well? He was the leader of the Aramaic-speaking Christians at Jerusalem. Finally, both the first century Jewish historian Josephus and the early Christian tradition state that James the Lord's brother was a faithful observer and stout defender of Jewish laws and ceremonies. No trace of such ritual emphasis occurs in this epistle.

These facts could suggest that the epistle was written late in the first century or early in the second. The writer may have been another James, or an admirer of James the Lord's brother who knew of his upright life and spoke in his name to insist that all Christians must imitate such obedience to God's will. Part of his reason for writing may well have been that some people in his day were making a false use of Paul's teaching to encourage moral laxity.

A Call to Sincere Faith and Life

Every line of this writing makes sense. It rebukes and corrects superficial living and pious pretenses. In it we find sound direction for daily life. It does not tell all that Christ has done for the Christian, nor does it present the full Christian faith and hope. But it makes clear what God rightly expects of those who say they believe in Christ.

It does not belittle faith. Indeed, it emphasizes it, and insists that prayer must be offered in the faith that God will hear and answer it (James 1: 6). It urges men to pray in all the situations of life, whether pleasant or trying. It appeals to men to pray for one another (James 5: 16). All this clearly rests upon confident faith in God. But this faith, when genuine, results in trust in God, in self-control, in friendship and helpfulness. This epistle does not want less faith; it wants faith to be the real thing and to result in dedication of the entire life. To talk about faith is never enough.

The epistle does not belittle Christ. Jesus is the Christ, and he is "our Lord," "the Lord of glory" (James 2: 1). He will be the judge of men (James 5: 7, 8). Plainly, then, Christ is central for this writer. But he insists that we honor Christ, not by words and public poses, but by a life that is like that of the Master, who "went about doing good" (Acts 10: 38).

The epistle does not contradict Paul. It does not say things as he would, but there is no basic conflict. Paul kept insisting that we do not earn our standing with God. Because we sin, we need forgiveness. If we had to keep a law so perfectly as to earn our reward, we should be lost. But God meets our need. He sent Christ to do for us what we could not do for ourselves. Through Christ he offers us free forgiveness for our sin and release from the grip of evil. Yet Paul himself expected those who received this great gift to "walk in newness of life" (Rom. 6: 4). The faith he meant was not an idle outward profession that yielded no fruit in good living; it was, rather, "faith working through love" (Gal. 5: 6).

The trouble was that too many people listened when Paul said that God forgives sin, but failed to take him seriously when he called for love and newness of life. Evidently some wrongly used Paul's gospel to excuse lax living in the Church.

Their faith was a mere verbal show. It did not take hold of their lives.

For that reason The Epistle of James speaks out so sharply. Faith that is mere talk, that claims to believe but shows no change in life, is a fraud. "Show me your faith apart from your works, and I by my works will show you my faith" (James 2: 18). Man cannot save himself; so Paul said, and there is no reason to think that this writer would differ. But when God saves a man, it is by a faith so real that it controls the life of the believer. Something happens if the faith is real. A live faith produces good living. "Faith without works is dead."

READING HINTS: Read the epistle at one sitting and notice what dangers to Christian living are emphasized. Great passages include: the Christian triumph over trials (James 1: 2-15); Christian worship without class distinctions (James 2: 1-13); "faith without works is dead" (James 2: 14-26); the danger in misuse of the tongue (James 3: 1-12); remember that life is in God's hands (James 4: 13-17).

Verses Worth Knowing: James 1: 5, 12, 22, 27; 2: 1, 26; 3: 17; 4: 8, 10, 17; 5: 16, 19, 20.

CHAPTER 20

The First Letter of Peter

AGAIN a New Testament writer speaks of "the fiery ordeal which comes upon you to prove you" (I Peter 4: 12). Why do these books so often refer to hardship and persecution? The Christians were challenging the way that men lived and thought. Had the Jews accepted Christ, it would have made a radical change in their inherited worship and thinking. The Gentile world would have had to change even more. The Empire had its gods, and even thought its rulers divine. Each city, each guild of workmen, each social group had its gods, and so did most households. The Christians made a bold attack upon this pagan world. They told men that they "were in bondage to beings that by nature are no gods" (Gal. 4: 8), and so should turn "to God from idols, to serve a living and true God" (I Thess. 1: 9).

Most men in the pagan world resented this rebuke and challenge. They fought back. Some, to be sure, believing in many gods, did not object if the Christians wanted to add another. But others saw rightly that the new faith had an unyielding intolerance. There would be no room for the old religions if men accepted the Christian faith in "one God, the Father, from whom are all things and for whom we exist, and one Lord, Jesus Christ, through whom are all things and through whom we exist" (I Cor. 8: 6). Such a faith would destroy the pagan form of religious, civic, social, and political life. So the Christians were persecuted as a dangerous group.

Persecution in Asia Minor

First Peter reflects such a crisis. The gospel had spread widely in Asia Minor, and the letter went to all but the southern strip of that region. In some of these provinces Paul had preached, but he never went to Pontus, Bithynia, and Cappadocia. Did Peter preach there? We have no clear proof that he did, but the letter implies that at least he knew what these churches now faced.

In this entire area persecution now threatened the Christians. Who led the attack? Was it Roman officials or local groups who resented the growth of the Church? Most likely local agitators were stirring up the trouble. The letter puts no blame on the rulers, and expresses some hope that by loyalty to rulers and daily good living the Christians will silence slander (I Peter 2: 13-17). If an official decree had already condemned the Christians, good behavior would not have saved them. So the hostility of the common people or of self-appointed agitators seems to have caused the danger.

When did this crisis occur? Since the letter names Peter as writer, we at once look to the early 60's, for Peter was probably put to death at Rome in A.D. 64 (or 67). But a difficulty arises. We know of no general attack, either popular or official, against Christians in Asia Minor at that time. Nero persecuted Christians at Rome in the 60's, but nothing proves that these attacks spread beyond Rome. Perhaps, though, they did.

Thirty years later the Empire appears to have taken stern action against Christians in Asia Minor. The book of The Revelation comes out of that crisis. But this was an official attack. The threat of unofficial ill-treatment such as First Peter expects may well have arisen in the 60's.

A Letter from Rome

To these churches now forced to face trial Peter sends words of faith and encouragement. He writes "by" or "through"

Silvanus (I Peter 5: 12). This is probably the Silvanus or Silas who earlier had helped Paul (Acts 15: 40; I Thess. 1: 1; II Thess. 1: 1). Both the Gospels and ancient tradition tell us that Peter's native tongue was Aramaic. While he knew some Greek, he likely had trouble writing smooth Greek. For this reason Silvanus did more than write down what Peter dictated. He had a real part in expressing Peter's thought in good Greek, and this will explain why some parts of First Peter resemble the letters of Paul.

Peter writes from "Babylon" (I Peter 5: 13). This seems to mean Rome. As in the book of The Revelation (ch. 14: 8; 18: 2, 10, 21), "Babylon" appears to be a cryptic reference to the great capital city of the pagan world. So Peter writes from Rome, and the church there sends greetings to "the exiles of the dispersion" in Asia Minor (I Peter 1: 1). By "exiles" he means the Christians. The Jewish "Dispersion," that is, Jews living in Gentile lands, felt that they were out of place and away from their true home, which would be in the land of Israel. Just so the Christians, living in the midst of a pagan and hostile population, felt like strangers in a foreign land, and so Peter describes them as "exiles of the dispersion."

A Living and Sure Hope

To these threatened Christians, Peter speaks no word of defeat or discouragement. The key word of the letter is *hope* (I Peter 1: 3). This hope does not rest upon the greatness of the Christians; faced by trial, they feel inadequate. Nor does it rest upon help from government or public opinion; they offer no promise of safety and peace. Yet Christian hope is far more than a frantic wish that things may improve.

It is a confident hope with a solid basis. It rests upon God, in whose faithfulness, power, and mercy man can put full trust. It rests upon what God has done and has promised to do. His prophets promised that God would save man. In Jesus Christ, crucified but raised from the dead, he has begun to fulfill his good purpose. He will certainly finish his work, and those who by faith already know his forgiveness and power can stand fast in hope (I Peter 1: 3-12). In what God has done through Christ and is doing through the Spirit they find every reason to be confident.

Life in the Church

This hope yields good results in present life. It leads to reverence before God and to love for fellow Christians (I Peter 1: 13-25). Every true Christian turns from evil ways and gladly shares the life of the Church, which is "a spiritual house" whose members are "a chosen race, a royal priesthood, a holy nation, God's own people" (I Peter 2: 1-10). They all live in mutual helpfulness and in "humility toward one another" that grows out of humble trust in God (I Peter 5: 1-11). Even if persecution threatens, they refuse to be intimidated and frightened into silence; they openly witness to what God has done for them; they "declare the wonderful deeds of him who called you out of darkness into his marvelous light" (I Peter 2: 9).

This task all Christians share. The "priesthood" here mentioned is not a small minority of Christians. The New Testament never speaks of a human priesthood that stands between the other Christians and God and has strict power to grant or withhold the mercies of God. In the letter to the Hebrews the one high priest is Christ the Son, who ministers in heaven for all believers; no other priest is recognized. In First Peter the entire Church is to serve Christ and witness to the world. All serve; all witness, especially by their lives; each may help the others; there are elders to lead, and they should serve faithfully (I Peter 5: 1-3), but no man is entitled to stand between the Christian and Christ his Lord. First Peter clearly teaches the basic Protestant principle of "the priesthood of all believers." It allows no priestly hierarchy to stand between the believer and Christ.

Life in the World

How shall the Christian meet hostile criticism? He dare not share the passions and sins of the pagan world. Instead, his good conduct must be his answer to slanderous attacks (I Peter 2: 11, 12). He must honor and obey the lawful authorities in government and society (I Peter 2: 13-17). Christian slaves were to give good service even to cruel pagan masters. Such submissive, faithful service was the one way in which they could witness for Christ to their owners. If they had to suffer for their faith at the hands of such masters, it would comfort them to recall that Christ suffered too (I Peter 2: 18-25).

So, too, pure and upright living, and faithfulness in the home, was the one way in which a Christian wife of a pagan husband could hope to win her husband to Christ (I Peter 3: 1-6). Her one true ornament was to be "the imperishable jewel of a gentle and quiet spirit." A Christian husband was to live with love and courteous kindness toward his wife (I Peter 3: 7), and all Christians were to have "unity of spirit, sympathy, love of the brethren, a tender heart and a humble mind." They were never to "return evil for evil," but to "turn away from evil and do right" (I Peter 3: 8-12).

Facing Persecution

Now that suffering threatens the Church (I Peter 3: 13 to 4: 19), how are the Christians of Asia Minor to face it? Peter asks them to remember six things: (1) Be careful to do what is right; this should make hostile men more friendly (I Peter 3: 13). (2) If you must suffer, be sure that you do not deserve it; see that you only "suffer for doing right" (I Peter 3: 17). (3) Christ was faithful in suffering and came through to triumph; if you must suffer for the name of Christ, God will bless you even in that hard experience (I Peter 3: 18; 4: 13-16). (4) When pagans are hostile because you refuse to share in their evil living, stand firm by the will of God (I Peter 4: 1-4).

(5) The time of suffering will be short; the end of the age may be close at hand (I Peter 4: 7). (6) Since the end is coming, and every man must face God's judgment, fear the condemnation of God far more than the ill-treatment of men (I Peter 4: 17-19; compare I Peter 1: 17). God is a holy God; men must do his will.

Christ "the Chief Shepherd"

Christ is made as central for faith in First Peter as in every other New Testament writing. God had always planned for Christ's coming and ministry for men (I Peter 1: 20). When he came and suffered in the flesh, his suffering was not for any wrong that he did, for he was "without blemish." It was for man's good; he "died for sins" in order "that he might bring us to God" and so ransom men from their "futile ways" (I Peter 4: 1; 3: 18; 1: 18, 19).

But he rose from the dead, and through his resurrection gave men "a living hope" (I Peter 1: 3). He is now "the Shepherd and Guardian of your souls," "the chief Shepherd." So no Christian should shrink from the fellowship of suffering with him. All should rather "reverence Christ as Lord," sure that his kindly care will lead them to final happiness and security. For at the end of this age all men will see the full triumph of Christ (I Peter 2: 25; 5: 4; 3: 15; 1: 7, 13).

But what will be the final lot of those who lived before Christ came? Can they share in the life that he brings? The other New Testament writers give no answer to this question. But Peter declares that Christ, evidently between his death and resurrection, went and preached to the spirits of the dead. He thinks in particular of the sinful men of the long past days of Noah, on whom God brought the flood to punish their wickedness. They are outstanding examples of the much larger group to whom Christ preached (I Peter 3: 19, 20; 4: 6).

In this idea it appears once more how central Christ is for the writer. Every generation shares the same need of divine redemption and help. All will find the answer to their need in Christ. He is the central figure of history and all men will finally face him. But exactly how God has offered Christ's help to others is not our main concern. Our task is to be grateful for what he has given us, and to be faithful and active in the Christian life of love that is steadied by hope.

"Be Prepared to Make a Defense"

The world today seems quite different from that in which First Peter was written. Yet cynics still ridicule Christians; men belittle and reject Christ; in recent years believers of many lands have suffered for their loyal faith. For all of us and at all times, this life is a battleground between the pagan world and the way of Christ. So the lines of First Peter still speak a vital message. The gospel still gives us the faith and the living hope by which we can stand steadfast and live in love.

"Now for a little while you may have to suffer various trials" and be "tested by fire." But "have no fear of them, nor be troubled, but in your hearts reverence Christ as Lord. Always be prepared to make a defense to any one who calls you to account for the hope that is in you, yet do it with gentleness and reverence; and keep your conscience clear, so that, when you are abused, those who revile your good behavior in Christ may be put to shame. For it is better to suffer for doing right, if that should be God's will, than for doing wrong. . . . Above all hold unfailing your love for one another, since love covers a multitude of sins. . . . Humble yourselves therefore under the mighty hand of God, that in due time he may exalt you. Cast all your anxieties on him, for he cares about you."

Reading Hints: Study in particular the passages on hope (I Peter 1: 3-9, 13, 21; 3: 15; 4: 13; 5: 10); on Jesus Christ and his work (I Peter 1: 3, 7, 11, 13, 18-21; 2: 21-25; 3: 15, 18-22; 4: 1, 13; 5: 1, 4); on the Church as the equal brotherhood of God's own people (I Peter 2: 4-10); on suffering for being a Christian (I Peter 3: 13 to 4: 19).

Verses to Think of Again: I Peter 1: 3, 15, 22; 2: 9, 12, 15-17; 3: 8, 9, 13-17; 4: 8, 10; 5: 6, 7.

CHAPTER 21

Jude and Second Peter

A SERIOUS THREAT to the purity and strength of the Church led to the writing of Jude and Second Peter. Misguided men were teaching that gross physical indulgence does not harm the Christian at all. They were living in a shamelessly immoral way.

The Body and the Soul

Back of this dangerous teaching was the view that the body and all physical things are completely separate from the spiritual side of man. The false teachers who delighted to live immoral lives had taken up such teaching and used it. They seem to have claimed that the Christian faith has to do only with man's soul. In that part of his life he should believe in Christ, and worship and serve him. But this faith does not concern the body and the physical things of the world. What we do with them does not affect our spiritual life.

If the physical and spiritual are separate, and neither can hurt or help the other, then man may choose one of two ways of life. He may become an ascetic; that is, to be a true Christian he may deny himself all normal physical pleasure and comfort. Since the body has no place in a true Christian life, it is really a hindrance. Its normal impulses actually tempt the spiritual man to do wrong things. So the believer should try to crush his physical impulses; he should indulge them as little as possible. He should eat sparingly, and avoid delicacies; he should avoid marriage because sex life is inherently evil. Indeed, since in such a view the body hinders good living, the soul's separation from it at death will be a liberation and benefit.

The other way to live, if matter and spirit have nothing in common, is to indulge the body and enjoy physical pleasures without restraint. Those who thus thought claimed that even sexual immorality does not harm the spiritual life. So they committed adultery, broke up homes, and showed their supposed independence of usual moral standards.

"A Temple of the Holy Spirit"

Neither of these two views is Christian. Self-discipline is right, but asceticism is wrong. God made the world. He made the body, and so it is not an evil thing. "And God saw everything that he had made, and, behold, it was very good" (Gen. 1: 31). "The earth is the Lord's, and the fulness thereof; the world, and they that dwell therein" (Ps. 24: 1). He made man, the entire man, body, soul, and spirit. Therefore the body can be, and for the Christian it is, the "temple of the Holy Spirit." "So glorify God in your body" (I Cor. 6: 19, 20). It is the Christian's duty to present his body "as a living sacrifice, holy and acceptable to God" (Rom. 12: 1).

Self-discipline is right; immoral indulgence is wrong. Just as the Christian faith rejects asceticism and its view that normal physical life is unavoidably degrading, so it emphatically condemns the libertine view that one may indulge the body in any way one wishes.

Man is not two separate beings. He is one person. His body, mind, and soul are all parts of one human life. Modern psychology recognizes that fact. The body and mind interact. Every good doctor knows this. The faith and mental attitude of a man have ties with his physical condition. The Bible knew that centuries ago. Indulgent and immoral living in the body is coupled with an indulgent and immoral attitude in the heart of man. When the body does wrong, man is a sinner. Real faith dedicates body, mind, and soul to God in one complete loyalty.

Plainly, then, the Early Church could not tolerate those who practiced and defended shamelessly immoral living. To accept such low standards would doom the Church. All through the New Testament we hear its demand for purity of life, for discipline of mind and body. It offers God's forgiveness to those who have taken the wrong way and now want to turn to him and do right. It invites men to accept God's grace in faith and respond by dedicating their lives to him. But this offers no hope to those who propose to continue in sin. Lax living, openly paraded and defended, finds only condemnation.

The Epistle of Jude

The Epistles of Jude and Second Peter join in denouncing this libertine way of life. Both are general epistles; they are addressed to all Christians. They were not written to a single church or a limited region, but were to be distributed and read wherever Christians were found.

Jude is the shorter. It concentrates on this one theme. The writer had planned a longer, more general work, but decided that he must at once write to condemn those who were boldly introducing and shamelessly defending immorality in the life of the Church (Jude 3, 4). When he tells his readers to "contend for the faith," he does not think of a general teaching of Christian truth; he means particularly the clear defense of the purity of the Church against those who say it does not matter how one lives in one's body. He declares that God's judgment will fall on such evil living, and he gives examples of such judgment from the history of Israel (Jude 5-13). Such corrupt and divisive living had been predicted and denounced by both Jewish and apostolic teachers (Jude 14-19).

To the readers the author says: "Keep yourselves in the love of God" by faith, by prayer, and by loyal obedience in the whole life. Be ready to help others to give up evil ways, but be careful not to get dragged down to that low level of life (Jude 20-23). The inspiring closing benediction makes it clear that God can and will help every sincere Christian to avoid falling into evil. By the power of God the believer can live a clean and wholesome life, to the praise of God and Christ (Jude 24, 25).

The author, according to ancient tradition, was Jude the brother of James and so of Jesus (Jude 1). So little is known of him that we cannot say certainly where he worked. The brothers of the Lord were in the Church from early days (Acts 1: 14; I Cor. 9: 5), and Jude may have lived to see the rise of the evil teaching here opposed.

It is not clear just when or where this epistle was written. It could not have been written before the closing decades of the first century, for it looks back to the now past days of the apostles (Jude 17). The Church hesitated about including it in the New Testament. One reason was that Jude 9 refers to a writing called the Assumption of Moses and Jude 14 quotes the Book of Enoch. Neither of these books is to be found in the Old Testament. Many seem to have felt that a book that quotes such non-Biblical writings could not be of the highest rank. In time, however, the Church found that the epistle's vigorous teaching gave a needed witness to the original Christian gospel, and the hesitation faded away.

The Second Epistle of Peter

Second Peter is longer than Jude, and its second chapter closely parallels Jude. It condemns false teachers who try to excuse base, immoral behavior. It predicts certain divine judgment on such teaching and living. "These, like irrational animals, creatures of instinct," "who indulge in the lust of defiling passion and despise authority," "bring in destructive heresies, even denying the Master who bought them, bringing upon themselves swift destruction" (II Peter 2: 12, 10, 1). That is, those who live thus do wrong; they deny Christ, by what they do as well as by what they teach; they are not really Christians, for Christians dedicate body and mind and spirit to the pure service of their Master.

In II Peter, ch. 1, the writer, to prepare for the facing of this issue, has reminded the readers that God has given men all the gifts and help they need for good and reverent living (II Peter 1: 3, 4). He urges godliness, brotherly affection, and love. These are the marks of the true Christian life. They make life fruitful for good (II Peter 1: 5-11). Each Christian should work to show these marks; "be the more zealous to confirm your call and election" (II Peter 1: 10). This is not new teaching; it rests back upon the witness of Peter, who had close personal companionship with Jesus (II Peter 1: 12-18), and it is also the witness of the prophets (II Peter 1: 19-21).

In II Peter, ch. 3, the certainty of God's judgment on immoral living is stressed. Some Christians had ceased to expect this judgment; they no longer looked for the end of the world. It had been promised; they had expected it soon; when it delayed, they decided that they need not fear judgment. The writer declares that man cannot know when God will act; his measures of time are not ours. But the end will come; God will judge evil; the end will come "like a thief," and Christians should always be ready for it. It will bring a new and righteous order in which God's people will live. In it evil will have no place (II Peter 3: 1-13).

Some Christians had used Paul's teaching about God's free grace to excuse immoral living. This had happened even during Paul's lifetime (Rom. 3: 8), and he had denounced such shameful distortion of the gospel. He had preached forgiveness to every person who sincerely repents, but he gave no hope for the brazen wrongdoer who complacently continues to do evil. The writer grants that some things in Paul's letters are hard to understand, but he insists that only by malicious twisting of what Paul says can anyone get from him support for such bad living. Those who thus twist Paul also misinterpret the rest of the Scripture. The readers should reject such trickery, keep steadfast in Christian faith and action, and "grow in the grace and knowledge of our Lord and Savior Jesus Christ" (II Peter 3: 14-18).

The date of Second Peter cannot be early. Careful comparison of II Peter, ch. 2, with Jude indicates that the two passages are related, and that Jude is the earlier. By a method of writing then in use, Second Peter takes over and uses material that Jude had presented at an earlier time.

Other facts confirm the late date. The letters of Paul, it appears, have not only been collected, but are already accepted as authoritative, for after referring to them the writer speaks of "the *other* scriptures" (II Peter 3: 16). This implies that the letters too are Scripture, a situation that came several decades at least after Paul's death. In the time of Paul, the term "Scripture" referred to our Old Testament. Then, too, the complaint that the end of the world has long been delayed points to a late date (II Peter 3: 4). The same conclusion is suggested by the fact that no ancient Christian writer mentions Second Peter until the third century; only then, and slowly, does the Church decide to accept it.

All this means that since Peter died when Paul did, or about the same time, he could not have written this epistle. Some later Christian, deeply concerned over the moral laxity that threatened the Church, wrote as an admirer of Peter and as he was confident Peter would have spoken had he been alive. This may have been between A.D. 100 and 150, although a date slightly earlier is possible.

The Christian Moral Standard

Jude and Second Peter drive home the truth that upright moral living is an essential part of the Christian life. To be sure, the entire New Testament, and the Old Testament as well, teaches that the whole life must be subject to God. But these two epistles, written when moral laxity was trying to claim a place of respect in the Church, rightly put special stress on the necessity of pure and wholesome living.

The Church always needs this clear reminder. Because it teaches that God freely forgives sin and that man never earns God's grace, some may be tempted to think that God does not care how they live. They may think that Christian freedom is freedom to do as they please, to live lives of indulgence, to cast off self-discipline of the body. But that is not Christian freedom. The freedom God gives is freedom from the tyranny of self-centered living and coarse self-indulgence; it is freedom to do right, freedom to dedicate the whole self to the service of God and the helping of other people. Jude and Second Peter remind us that no teaching is Christian that defends lax moral standards; no life is Christian that is content with physical dissipation and indulgence.

Reading Hints: Read each of these epistles at one sitting. Compare carefully Jude 4-23, and II Peter, ch. 2, to see how many words and ideas they share.

Noteworthy Verses on Christian Living: Jude 20, 21, 24, 25; II Peter 1: 3, 5-8, 10, 11, 21; 3: 9, 13, 18.

CHAPTER 22

The Three Letters of John

TRUE FAITH leads to right living. On this fact every New Testament writer insists. Paul, for example, not only offered the grace of God in Christ but also expected the "fruit of the Spirit" in daily life. The Epistle of James declared that "faith without works is dead." In Jude and Second Peter we again find strong emphasis on this close tie between faith and action.

The same truth comes out in the three Epistles of John. Written in or near Ephesus, at the close of the first century, they attack false teaching and harmful leaders that threatened the health of the Church. The trouble was not the brazen immorality that Jude and Second Peter so vigorously denounced. Yet the same idea, that physical life and spiritual loyalty are entirely separate, was back of the new difficulties. It led to false teaching about Christ; it was causing a split in the Church. Four great errors of thought and life resulted.

To combat these errors one alert Christian leader wrote the three Epistles of John. He never names himself, but the language, style, and ideas, as well as the ancient Church tradition, show that one man wrote all three, and that he also wrote the Gospel of John. He twice calls himself "the elder" (II John 1; III John 1). The very fact that he uses only this title and does not need to give his name shows that he was a prominent leader. He could utter the needed warning against the false ideas that threatened the Church; he also could give a clear statement of the truth, so that no room for such harmful ideas would remain.

"Jesus Christ Has Come in the Flesh"

First of all, some were teaching that Jesus had not come in the flesh, that he never had a physical human body. Of course, if all matter is evil and nothing physical can have a wholesome place in Christian life, then for Jesus to have a physical body would have dragged him down into evil. In that view, it would free him from criticism to show that he never had a body of flesh and blood. So some taught that he only "seemed" to have a body like ours and live a physical life. Such teaching was called "Docetism," from a Greek word which means "seem."

But this teaching, intended to protect Jesus from criticism and make him greater, failed of its purpose. It made his earthly life mere make-believe and deception. It was not real; it no longer gave men an example to follow. It reduced his death, which he had accepted in loyalty to his work and for the benefit of men, to a hollow pretense. Thus the entire gospel story lost its meaning and appeal.

No wonder the writer of these epistles fights so unworthy a view of Christ. "Many deceivers have gone out into the world, men who will not acknowledge the coming of Jesus Christ in the flesh" (II John 7). But the first disciples actually heard, saw, and touched the real Jesus, who, even though he was the Son of God, lived a truly human life (I John 1: 1-3). The Church cannot surrender the fact that he "became flesh and dwelt among us" in a real life that was "full of grace and truth" (John 1: 14). He came "to take away sins, and in him there is no sin" (I John 3: 5).

Right here, in fact, was part of the unique strength of the gospel. Other religions had their myths about the doings of their gods. But such things never happened. In contrast, the Christian message tells of a Lord who has lived a real life and "in every respect has been tempted as we are, yet without sinning" (Heb. 4: 15). There is power and appeal in this good example and moral triumph of Jesus. The "elder" knew that here the Church has God-given truth; "every spirit which confesses that Jesus Christ has come in the flesh is of God" (I John 4: 2).

"He . . . Will Forgive Our Sins and Cleanse Us"

A second fault of misguided Christians was the lack of a sense of sin. Perhaps here again the idea was at work that physical life has no connection with Christian faith, that what happens in the body cannot hurt the spiritual life. Certainly the writer noticed that some felt no need of forgiveness.

Such people were making their task too simple. We are responsible for what we do. Our responsibility covers not only the thoughts and purposes of our minds—and who is not at fault here?—but also all our physical actions and social relations. We may deceive ourselves, but we never deceive God. "If we say we have no sin, we deceive ourselves, and the truth is not in us. If we confess our sins, he is faithful and just, and will forgive our sins and cleanse us from all unrighteousness. If we say we have not sinned, we make him a liar" (I John 1: 8-10).

"We . . . Ought to Love One Another"

Still a third serious fault was that these self-confident persons felt quite superior to other Christians. In their pride they thought that the common Christians were sadly inferior. So they did not love their fellow Christians; they looked down upon them. Some, it seems, withdrew from the Church to form their own little group; they were too good, they thought, to worship, eat, and live with ordinary Christians (I John 2: 19).

The elder protested with all his power against such divisive pride. The very nature of the Christian life is love. In this love it reflects the attitude of God himself. "Love is of God. . . . In this the love of God was made manifest among us, that God sent his only Son into the world, so that we might live through him." From him we learn how to live. "Beloved, if God so loved us, we also ought to love one another. . . . If any one says, 'I love God,' and hates his brother, he is a liar. . . . He who loves God should love his brother also" (I John 4: 7, 9, 11, 20, 21).

"He Who Does Good Is of God"

The fourth fault that the elder exposed was putting too much emphasis on knowledge and not enough on doing the will of God. No human being, of course, is in danger of knowing too much. But we may emphasize facts and ideas so much that mere knowledge seems enough. If we do that, we miss the tremendous importance of doing what God wants men to do. Men are not saved merely by knowing facts. As the Form of Government of the Presbyterian Church says, "Truth is in order to goodness." Truth is for the sake of goodness. It must be harnessed to life to do what it was intended to do. "Do not imitate evil but imitate good. He who does good is of God; he who does evil has not seen God" (III John 11).

No other way of life has a real future. "He who does the will of God abides forever. . . . No one who does not do right is of God, nor any one who does not love his brother. . . . Let us not love in word or speech but in deed and in truth" (I John 2: 17; 3: 10, 18). The writer does not tell, in such detail as Jesus and Paul do, what it means to do the will of God. But he does stress the one great thing that proud people are missing; he calls them to show genuine love to all their fellow Christians.

A General Letter

The First Epistle of John is much longer than the two brief letters that follow. It does not begin or end as does the usual letter. Nor is it addressed to any local church. It states in a general way important Christian truth, which Church leaders can copy and carry wherever Christians deny the true humanity of Jesus and fail to show brotherly love.

It declares that the Son of God really came into a true human life, that he died for men's good, that God's love was shown in his coming and death, and that he continues to intercede with the Father on behalf of every sincere believer (I John 1: 7; 2: 1, 2; 3: 5; 4: 2, 10). But it demands with equal urgency that the Christian love his brother believer (I John 4: 20). These two leading points are combined in a verse that sums up what First John would teach: "This is his commandment, that we should believe in the name of his Son Jesus Christ and love one another, just as he has commanded us" (I John 3: 23).

A Letter to a Local Church

Second John says in briefer form what First John has already stated. It adds one point: Christians should not show hospitality to those who are spreading false teaching about Christ; those who entertain false teachers must share responsibility for such teaching (II John 7-11).

The letter appears at first reading to be addressed to a Christian "lady and her children." This, however, is very likely a way of referring to a specific church—just where we cannot say—and its members. If this is so, the closing verse means that the church from which the elder writes sends greetings to the church he addresses.

A Letter to a Loyal Christian

Third John deals with a problem of leadership. The elder obviously had wide influence; he sent messengers to churches to help them. The Christians were still a small minority. Church organization was not clearly fixed. No church papers gave news of other Christians and so bound the churches together. Instead, traveling leaders and their helpers did much to hold the churches together in a unity of interest and spirit. Letters from leaders also helped in this, as Paul's writings prove. Like him, the elder sent messengers and wrote letters to churches.

But in one church, probably in Asia Minor, his leadership was opposed. Diotrephes, evidently a local leader in that church, determined to keep it independent. He rejected the elder's authority. He refused to receive traveling Christians who represented the elder, and forbade any other Christian to entertain them. If anyone did receive them, Diotrephes put him out of the church. As the elder says, he "likes to put himself first" (III John 9).

To check the ambition and dictatorial ways of Diotrephes, the elder writes to his friend Gaius, a member of the same church. He urges Gaius, who has a splendid reputation as a good Christian (III John 3), to befriend the elder's messengers. Demetrius, it appears, carries the letter, or in some way helps the elder in his work (III John 12).

Diotrephes may have thought that strong local leadership would be better for the church than occasional visits and letters from leaders living elsewhere. But the elder may well have had reason to suspect that sympathy with false teaching was back of Diotrephes' hostility. So he hoped to follow his letter with a visit. In this church, as in the others he served, he wanted to keep alive the loyalty to Christ, the love of fellow Christians, and the steady Christian living that are the marks of the true disciple.

The Family of Faith

Common to all three of these writings is the theme of Christian fellowship. We have fellowship with God the Father through Jesus Christ (I John 1: 3). It is our privilege not only to know about him, but to believe in him, trust him, and serve him in worship and life.

We have fellowship with fellow Christians in our local church. He who thinks himself too good to share in this common worship and mutual helpfulness has a badly distorted view of himself. And he has not understood the good that comes from others. All are imperfect, but as all seek the grace and help of God, each can also help the other and each needs the others. The basis of great thinking and great vision is not neglect of the local group, but loyal sharing in the life of that local fellowship.

We have fellowship with other Christians in the world. We may keep in touch with them by letters and writings, by sympathy and imagination, by prayer for them which is matched by their prayer for us. The local church is not an isolated island in a blank sea of loneliness. It is a member of a world-wide brotherhood whose common faith gives courage and strength to all as they work together to serve their common Lord.

Reading Hints: In reading I John, notice: (1) what the elder says about Jesus Christ; (2) what he says about sin and what Christ does for our sin; (3) what he says about the necessity of brotherly love; (4) what he says about the absolute necessity of doing the will of God.

Great Passages to Study: I John 1: 5 to 2: 6; 3: 11-18; 4: 7-21; 5: 1-5, 11-13.

What picture of the Church do you get from II John if "the elect lady and her children" means the local church and its members whom the elder is addressing, and "your elect sister" (II John 13) means the church where the writer is staying?

In III John, for what does the elder praise Gaius and blame Diotrephes?

CHAPTER 23

The Book of The Revelation

DOES THE CHURCH FACE DEFEAT? More than once hostile attacks have tempted Christians to ask this question. At times persecution and at other times the clever attempt of the State to use the Church for political purposes have threatened the Christian cause.

The first question leads to others: Does God face defeat? Will the work of Christ fail in the end? Will evil win? Will the good be crushed? Will the gospel message of God's saving purpose and power prove at last a cruel deception?

IS THE EMPEROR GOD?

Long ago the Church faced a test of its faith in God's victory. At the end of the first century a crisis confronted the Christians. The demand was made that people in the Roman Empire worship the emperor. This worship was zealously promoted in Asia Minor. It had its temples, priests, and special rites. It was a strong expression of patriotism, but it went beyond that to claim that the emperor was divine and so must be worshiped as a god.

This view had been held for decades by some. Each emperor was declared divine after his death, and some Roman subjects paid divine honors to the emperor even while he was alive. One earlier emperor, Caligula (A.D. 37-41), insisted that he was a god. He almost caused a great slaughter of Jews because they, with their belief in one God, could not worship him as he demanded. He ordered his statue set up in the Temple at Jerusalem, and the Jews were ready to die first. Fortunately for them and for the honor of the Empire, Caligula died before the act was done, and the plans were dropped.

No other emperor made such an extreme claim until Domitian (A.D. 81-96). Toward the end of his reign he seems to have encouraged men to worship him as divine. He liked to be called "Lord and God." Indeed, the climax of the Gospel of John, which probably was written during Domitian's reign, may be a deliberate contradiction of the claims of the emperor. In John 20: 28, Thomas exclaims to the risen Christ, "My Lord and my God!" Not Domitian, but Christ, is the Lord whom the Christians honor as divine.

For many Roman subjects the emperor's claim raised no problem. They were already used to the worship of many gods. It was easy to worship one more. Others did not take the claim seriously. In their guilds, cities, and countries they found various gods worshiped. They regarded these practices as a mere form, and observed them as a social duty. They did not really believe in these gods.

"For Us There Is One God"

Christians could not worship the emperor or any other pagan gods, nor could they go through the outward forms of such worship. They were ready to respect the ruling powers, and they prayed for them (Rom. 13: 1-7; I Tim. 2: 1, 2). But they could not worship or pretend to worship the rulers as gods. "For us there is one God, the Father, from whom are all things and for whom we exist, and one Lord, Jesus Christ, through whom are all things and through whom we exist" (I Cor. 8: 6).

For this uncompromising attitude they were often attacked. They were called unpatriotic. Men declared that loyal Romans could not accept the Christian faith, and that Rome should not tolerate it (Acts 16: 21). Christians were even called enemies of society. Every group in social, business, and political life had its patron gods, and yet this new faith called men to turn "to God from idols, to serve a living and true God" (I Thess. 1: 9). Before long the Christians were even called atheists. To us this seems strange, but in the ancient world to believe in gods meant to share the community worship of the pagan deities, and this the Christians could not do.

The enemies of the early Christians were not blind. They saw that if they accepted the Christian faith, they would have to make radical changes in the political, business, and social life they knew. They would have to cancel emperor worship, reject all the pagan gods of the cities, guilds, and social groups, and stop all worship of idols. More than that, Christian faith would require them to rethink all the duties and relations of life. Everything would have to be related to the one God and his Christ; every phase of life would become a part of man's duty to this one God. Where Christ is accepted, life has a new center and standard, which will bring radical changes in government, business, and society. The enemies of the Early Church knew this. So, while they should have believed in Christ, they refused. To justify their refusal, they felt driven to oppose the Christians.

The result was open persecution. From the earliest days of the Church local outbursts of hostility occurred. But these were not due to official imperial action. Even when Nero, in A.D. 64, cruelly killed numerous Christians at Rome, on false charges that they had set fire to the city, he did not, as far as we know, extend the persecution to other regions. But under Domitian wider persecution occurred. It became most acute in Asia Minor. Antipas, a faithful Christian, was put to death at Pergamum (Rev. 2: 13). The vision of "those who had been slain for the word of God and for the witness they had borne" (Rev. 6: 9) suggests that many unnamed Christians had suffered. Faced with the choice between emperor worship or martyrdom, they chose to die rather than betray their faith.

John to the Persecuted Church

The book of The Revelation was written when this persecution, which so far had been limited, threatened to become systematic and universal. The writer, John, it appears, had himself suffered some for his faith. He was "on the island called Patmos on account of the word of God and the testimony of Jesus" (Rev. 1: 9). This could mean that he was there to preach the gospel. But twice later he uses the same expression to refer to persecution (Rev. 6: 9; 20: 4). So very likely he had been exiled from his home in Asia Minor because officials there objected to his preaching. There at Patmos, off the west coast of Asia Minor, he was led, about A.D. 95, to write to the threatened churches in western Asia Minor.

Who was this John? According to the main ancient tradition, he was the apostle John. Another tradition, that the apostle John had been put to death at an earlier time, is not very strongly attested. So the way is open to say that the apostle John wrote this book late in life, after spending many years in Asia Minor as a Christian leader. In the book itself the writer says only that he, John, is a servant of Christ and a brother of the suffering Christians of Asia Minor (Rev. 1: 1, 9).

John writes to give comfort and courage to his hard-pressed fellow Christians. But he knows that the help they need does not come from man. He himself is only God's spokesman. The readers must put their trust in God. It was God who gave him the revelation, the message the book contains (Rev. 1: 1). That God has the power and authority to help men is the meaning of the impressive scene in heaven, where in vision John sees how God on his throne receives the worship and praise of all the ranks of angels (Rev., ch. 4). The majesty and power of this God are back of the Christians. He will keep them and no one can thwart his purpose to save them. He is the "Almighty" (Rev. 1: 8). This word, used but once in all the rest of the New Testament, occurs nine times in this book. The readers can feel safe in the care of their God, whose power cannot be successfully challenged.

In this work of God, Jesus Christ is the central figure. God gives the revelation to John through Christ (Rev. 1: 1, 19). In the scene in heaven (Rev., ch. 5), the Lamb stands in the center and with the Father receives the reverence even of the highest angels. He has died for men. He holds in his hand the power to rule the churches. He will defeat all evil forces and care for those who have to suffer; "the Lamb in the midst of the throne will be their shepherd" (Rev. 7: 17). He only can open for John the scroll of things to come.

The actual command to write came to John in a vision of the risen Christ (Rev. 1: 9-20). He appears to John, tells who he is, and directs John to write "what you see, what is and what is to take place hereafter" (Rev. 1: 19).

This opening vision calls attention to the nature of the entire book. It is full of vivid pictures and symbols. In this way of putting its message, it follows a pattern known from some of the latest Old Testament books and from other late Jewish writings. Such books appeared in times of hardship and persecution. Their Jewish writers used dramatic and symbolic language to reveal God's purpose to save his people soon. These books were known as "apocalypses"; that is, they uncovered or revealed things hidden from ordinary human knowledge. Similar to these writings is the book of The Revelation. By using symbolic and dramatic language, influenced by such earlier apocalyptic writings as the Old Testament Book of Daniel, the author sought to inspire and guide his oppressed readers. At the same time, the anti-Christian political powers could not find in his mysterious words a clear ground for seizing and condemning the author or those who used his book.

To see how true it is that the book of The Revelation puts what it has to say in a series of pictures, consider the ways in which it presents Jesus Christ. He appears here first as an impressive human figure in a long robe, walking among the seven golden lampstands that represent the churches; later he is described as a lion, a root, and a lamb; he also rides forth from heaven as a warrior on a white horse (Rev. 1: 13; 5: 5, 6; 19: 11). To combine all these pictures in one drawing is impossible, but each one means something. The robed figure represents the dignity, authority, and splendor of the risen Christ, who has the right to command the writer and the churches. The lion stands for his kingly power. The root indicates his Davidic descent. The lamb, the most frequent way of referring to Christ in this book, recalls especially his sacrificial death for men. The warrior figure points forward to his final, complete defeat of all evil forces. Each picture tells part of the truth about Christ.

These visions or pictures do not tell the story of all stages of world history. They give to God's people comfort in trial and assurance of rescue. The writer's aim was to say to these persecuted people that God's power will keep and finally save those who are faithful. Though they themselves are weak, and may suffer, God by Christ will bring them through to his eternal Kingdom.

Letters to the Seven Churches

But the gifts of God do not benefit those who do not hold to them. So John's great aim is to get his hard-pressed Christian friends to hold fast to their faith, no matter what the cost. He addresses seven churches. Perhaps they are the ones most threatened, or most in need of instruction. But they probably represent all the churches in danger.

These churches must first be strong in their own faith and life. Danger does not come merely from the outside. Inner weakness is perhaps the most deadly peril. So in Rev., chs. 2 and 3, the writer speaks of the strength or weakness of each of the seven churches. Three types emerge. Some are still strong and ready to suffer for their faith. Others have a rather good record, but either are losing some of their earlier steadiness and earnestness or are tolerating members that teach and practice immorality. Still others are weak; they need sharp rebuke and immediate reform to be able to stand fast in trial.

The purpose of John is clear. He urges the praiseworthy churches to hold firm; he seeks to lead the wavering churches to repent, renew their Christian faith, and stand fast in loyalty to Christ against all hostile attacks. The first need of the Church, its greatest hope under trial, is its inner strength and united brotherhood in common loyalty to Christ.

The Things to Come

The writer begins with the divine command to him to write, and tells of his vision of Christ, once crucified for men but now the risen Lord of the Church. He next rebukes and encourages the seven churches. Then he turns to "what is to take place hereafter." But he looks at the future in the light of the heavenly reign of God and Christ (Rev., chs. 4; 5); this is the ground of the confidence that the Church can have for the future. Then, in Rev., ch. 6, begins a series of visions that picture disaster for evil and promise relief to the faithful. Prominent are three series of seven plagues: the seven seals (Rev. 6: 1 to 8: 5), the seven trumpets (Rev. 8: 6 to 11: 19), and the seven bowls (Rev. 15: 1 to 16: 21). Other scenes are inserted in these series. What do these pictures of plagues and blessings say to the readers?

They declare that God's judgment on the evil and the cowardly is coming soon. Good and evil are in conflict. But the power to win is with God, and Christ, acting for the Father, will defeat and banish the evil.

Included among those condemned are not only vicious evil men but also "the cowardly, the faithless" (Rev. 21: 8). This condemnation and the repeated urging that Christians hold fast warn the readers that they may lose eternal privileges not only by outrageous wickedness but also by cowardly fear for physical safety. When ridiculed or mistreated, they dare not put physical safety or comfort above God's claim for their loyalty. There is no good future for the coward.

But inserted among these pictures of judgment are glimpses of the happiness and privilege of the faithful. God wants more than brilliant spurts of fair-weather Christian living. He wants his people, when tested, to stand fast without yielding ground. This is often the hardest thing that men are asked to do. When persecution comes and men must suffer for confessing Christ as their Lord, it is doubly hard to be faithful. But there are times when men must choose between faith and betrayal. They have a good example; Christ was "the faithful and true witness" (Rev. 3: 14); he did not run from danger or dodge the cross; he stood fast, suffered, and yet triumphed. The Christian, by the power of God, can do likewise. To encourage such faithfulness, the writer more than once describes the happiness and privilege of the faithful who come through persecution without denying Christ (Rev. 7: 9-17; 14: 1-5; 20: 4).

The Unavoidable Choice

In so trying a crisis some no doubt looked for an easy way out. They wished for a way to be loyal both to the emperor and to Christ. This writer insists that no such escape exists. In the pictures that begin with the appearance of the beast in Rev., ch. 13, John indicates that every person must receive the mark of the beast or the mark of the Lamb. That is, unless one is ready to stand firm for Christ and suffer, he will have to worship the beast as divine.

Who is this beast? The beast from the sea (Rev. 13: 1-10) is the Roman Empire, with its claim that men should worship its emperor. The beast from the land (Rev. 13: 11-17) seems to be the priesthood that promoted emperor worship. That the first beast has his center in Rome is indicated by the way Rev. 17: 9 refers to the evil woman. She is seated on seven hills, and Rome, as every reader knew, was the city built upon seven hills.

The demand to worship the emperor as divine put before the Christians an inescapable choice. They could yield, deny Christ, and worship the emperor, or they could stand fast and accept martyrdom if necessary. The crisis permitted no compromise. The time was at hand when every man must wear either the mark of the beast or the mark of the Lamb. He must make his decision for Satan or for God, for the beast or for Christ, for evil or for the right. The true Christian knows that his one controlling loyalty is to God through Christ; he will not worship the emperor; he cannot disown Christ the "King of kings and Lord of lords" (Rev. 19: 16). For he knows that Christ will defeat the beast; God's cause will win.

The Thousand Years with Christ

To the martyrs who give their lives for Christ a special privilege is promised (Rev. 20: 1-6). This passage, which speaks of a thousand years of safety and blessing, has caused much bitter dispute. Some take it to mean that at the end of the world, before the Final Judgment, all Christians will enjoy a thousand years of blessedness on earth with Christ. Others think that the "thousand years" refer to the whole period of the Church in this world, from the first century to the final day.

But this passage really says that the martyrs will have this special blessing. Rev. 20: 4 refers only to those who have died because they refused to receive the mark of the beast (and according to Rev. 13: 15, those who thus refused to worship the beast were to be put to death as martyrs).

It is unfortunate that this one short passage has caused so much dispute. Remember that the book of The Revelation is full of pictures. It does not give a literal account of history, but offers help to the first century Church as it faces a crisis. It encourages Christians to be faithful under persecution. It does this in Rev. 20: 1-6 by assuring them that God will bless those who must die to be true to Christ; he will take special care of them and give them special recognition.

The Time of the End

When will the end come? The writer repeatedly says that it will come quickly (Rev. 3: 11; 22: 7, 10, 12, 20). In other places he warns that Christ will come to judge unless the erring churches change their ways (Rev. 2: 5, 16; 3: 3). He earnestly hopes and expects that God will soon bring relief and victory to the troubled Church. In the meantime he is standing fast and urges his readers to do the same. Though he hopes that the end will come soon, he does not try to fix the exact time. That, he knows, is in the hands of God.

Some have tried to be more exact than he was. They have tried to say just when Christ will return and the world will end. Christ himself said that he did not know the time of the end and that the disciples were not to know it beforehand (Mark 13: 32; Acts 1: 7). But this has not satisfied some Christians. Dozens and dozens of times men have predicted just when Christ will come and this age will end. They all so far have been proved wrong.

The end will come sooner or later. We humans cannot say when this will happen. Until it does, the Christian has this clear advice from Paul: "It is required of stewards that they be found trustworthy" (I Cor. 4: 2). That is what the writer of the book of The Revelation wanted his Christian friends to be. They were to be faithful in the coming trial.

The end, we now know, will be much later than John expected it to be. But his basic appeal for steadfast loyalty to Christ is still vital. Given that, God will care for the rest. The future is in his hands He is God; his purpose will triumph; he will vindicate those who are true to him and give them eternal joy. They will be safe with him now and in all time to come.

"After this I looked, and behold, a great multitude which

no man could number, from every nation, from all tribes and peoples and tongues, standing before the throne and before the Lamb, clothed in white robes, with palm branches in their hands, and crying out with a loud voice, 'We owe our salvation to our God who sits upon the throne, and to the Lamb!'" "The kingdom of the world has become the kingdom of our Lord and of his Christ, and he shall reign for ever and ever." "To him who sits upon the throne and to the Lamb be blessing and honor and glory and might for ever and ever!"

READING HINTS: Put yourself as you read in the place of a Christian under the mighty Roman Empire and threatened by a persecution that has already begun. How then would this book help you?

Passages That Stand Out: the risen Christ commands John to write (Rev. 1: 9-20); the letters to the seven churches (Rev., chs. 2; 3); praise to God on his throne (Rev., ch. 4); praise to the Lamb, who can open the scroll of things to come (Rev., ch. 5); the final blessing of God's faithful people (Rev. 7: 9-17); the Final Judgment (Rev. 20: 11-15); the new Jerusalem (Rev., ch. 21); the river of life and the tree of life (Rev. 22: 1-5).